POOLEY'S
PILOT AIRCRAFT GUIDES

Handling Notes

Piper Warrior
PA28

Martyn Blunden

Nothing in this manual supersedes any UK or EU legislation, rules or CAA or EASA regulations or procedures and any operational documents issued by The Stationery Office, the Civil Aviation Authority, National Aviation Authorities, the manufacturers of aircraft, engines and systems, or by the operators of aircraft throughout the world. Note that as maps and chart are changed regularly, those extracts reproduced in this book must not be used for flight planning or flight operations.

Copyright 2022 © Pooleys Flight Equipment Limited

Pooleys Pilot Aircraft Guides – Piper Warrior PA28

ISBN 978-1-84336-112-1

First Edition 2007
Reprinted with amendments September 2016
Second Edition July 2017
Reprinted with amendments December 2019
Reprinted with amendments January 2022

Pooleys Flight Equipment Ltd
Elstree Aerodrome
Elstree
Hertfordshire
WD6 3AW
United Kingdom

Telephone: +44(0)20 8953 4870
Email: sales@pooleys.com
Website: www.pooleys.com

All rights reserved. No part of this publication may be reproduced in any material form (including photocopying or storing it in any medium by electronic means and whether or not transiently or incidentally to some of the use of this publication (without the written permission of the copyright owner) except in accordance with the provisions of the Copyright, Designs and Patents Act 1988 or under the terms of a licence issued by the Copyright Licensing Agency Limited, 90 Tottenham Court Road, London, England W1P 0LP. Applications for the copyright owner's written permission to reproduce any part of this publication should be addressed to the publisher.

Warning: The doing of an unauthorised act in relation to a copyright work may result in both a civil claim for damages and criminal prosecution.

Author - Martyn Blunden

Martyn Blunden is the CFI at a Flight Training Organistation and holds FIC, IRI and CPL instructor ratings. Originally he gained his PPL in 1978, which preceded many years flying in that capacity with a fair amount of farm strip flying. Martyn has a great depth of knowledge of engineering and training, although not exclusively aeronautical as he ran his own agricultural engineering business for 15 years. For a number of years he was an advisor or engineering training at the West Sussex College of Agriculture and sat on the National Council for Agricultural Engineering Education and Training. He is a member of the Honourable Company of Air Pilots (HCAP), which has a long history itself for contributions to the education, and training of pilots. For the past 30 years he has continued to work with young people as a youth worker in his spare time, introducing them to flying whenever possible.

Contributors

Our thanks to the following for their contributions to this title: Angela Yates.

Foreword

Flying is an art, sport, pastime, pleasure and profession. It has different meanings to different people and for some just a dream. I for one fell in love with flying at an early age after a short trip into the sky with a friend of a friend. Probably the way it happens for many people. Every penny was then saved to enable me to learn to fly at the local field, on Condors (a wood and fabric taildragger). Like many others I tried the RAF, but didn't get past the sergeant in the careers office "don't think you are from the right background old boy "sort of thing, which was still around in those days. British Airways at Hamble was of a similar attitude. With self-esteem a bit dented but still a great passion for flying I remained a private pilot for some years until I realised that my destiny really was as a professional pilot. I cannot deny it takes a lot of hard work to achieve and maintain a high standard but I still consider myself privileged to do the job I do. Dreams are often hard to realise and in flying we cannot escape the fact that it is costly. So, any way in which someone who is already in "the club" can help others to do likewise, even if it is just in the form of encouragement and valuable advice should be done with enthusiasm. As, I too was encouraged to write this book. There is nothing quite like a clubroom full of pilots for opinions! But out of that sometimes gems of wisdom do come. Flying really is an activity where one can benefit from the experience of others; my experience (apart from flying) lies in engineering. So I hope through the pages of this book I can pass on some of my knowledge that may help at some time. Also included is information that I have had passed on to me from my instructors in the past and that distilled from the flight manual. I hope that you find the information useful whether it be sport, pleasure or professional flying you indulge in. I would also like to thank my partner Helen for her help in putting together the draft document and for some of the diagrams that accompany the text.

The Aircraft and its Systems

Having a sound understanding of "what makes the aeroplane work", will equip the pilot with a better knowledge to deal with any malfunctions should they occur in flight. Better still; to spot a potential problem before it becomes an airborne dilemma. It is the intention of this guide to provide the pilot with the background information to assist in achieving the best and safest performance from the aircraft. Some basic engineering principles are also explained where it is thought appropriate, for the benefit of student pilots and those unfamiliar with the subject matter. Or, where a bit of revision would not go amiss!

However this document is not authoritative, as the only such document is the official Pilot's Operating Handbook/Flight Manual. Each aircraft has its own POH/FM that is amended for any single particular aircraft for variations in specification and country of operation. It is the POH of the aircraft you fly, that you should consult, for operational procedures, performance and safety matters in the interest of good airmanship.

In addition to the personal interest in how the aeroplane works, a pilot should also remember that in the UK the Air Navigation Order sets out in articles 69 & 73 legal pre-flight actions required of the commander of an aircraft in addition to the requirements of EASA Part NCO. This is reproduced here to remind us of our legal responsibilities as pilots even before we get airborne. Failure to comply with these or any other pertinent requirements could lead to legal prosecution should an incident or accident occur.

Article 69

69 Obilgations of Pilot-in-Command

(1) The pilot in command must only use aerodromes and operating sites that are adequate for the type of aircraft and operation concerned.

Flight preparation
(2) Before commencing a flight, the pilot in command must ascertain by every reasonable means available that the ground and water facilities, including communication facilities and navigation aids available and directly required on such a flight, for the safe operation of the aircraft, are adequate for the type of operation under which the flight is to be conducted.

Operating procedures
(3) The pilot in command must ensure that—
　(a) the flight is performed in such a way that the operating procedures specified in the flight manual, or where required the operations manual, for the preparation and execution of the flight are followed; and
　(b) procedures are established and followed for any reasonably foreseeable emergency situation.

Meteorological conditions
(4) The pilot in command must only commence or continue—
　(a) a Visual Flight Rules flight if—
　　(i) the latest available meteorological information indicates that the weather conditions along the route and at the intended destination aerodrome at the estimated time of use will be at or above the applicable Visual Flight Rules operating minima; and
　　(ii) the pilot in command has planned an alternative course of action to provide for the eventuality that the flight cannot be completed as planned because of weather conditions;
　(b) a flight under Instrument Flight Rules towards the planned destination aerodrome if the latest available meteorological information indicates that, at the estimated time of arrival, the weather conditions at the destination or at least one destination alternate aerodrome are at or above the applicable aerodrome operating minima notified, prescribed or otherwise designated by the relevant competent authority.

Selection of destination alternate aerodrome
(5) If, according to the information available, an aircraft would be required to be flown in accordance with the Instrument Flight Rules at the aerodrome of intended landing, the pilot in command of the aircraft must select before take-off a destination alternate aerodrome unless no aerodrome suitable for that purpose is available.
(6) A flight to be conducted in accordance with the Instrument Flight Rules to an aerodrome when no suitable destination alternate aerodrome is available must not be commenced by the pilot in command unless—
　(a) an instrument approach procedure notified, prescribed or otherwise designated by the relevant competent authority is available for the aerodrome of intended landing; and
　(b) available current meteorological information indicates that visual meteorological conditions will exist at the aerodrome of intended landing from two hours before until two hours after the estimated time of arrival.

Navigation and landing during loss of navigational capability
(7) The pilot in command must ensure that sufficient means are available to navigate and land at the destination aerodrome or at any destination alternate aerodrome in the case of loss of navigational capability for the intended approach and landing operation.

Airworthiness, equipment, baggage and cargo
(8) The pilot in command must ensure that—
   (a) the aircraft is airworthy;
   (b) instruments and equipment required for the execution of the flight are installed in the aircraft and are operative, unless operation with inoperative or missing equipment is permitted by the minimum equipment list or the CAA;
   (c) all equipment, baggage and cargo are properly loaded and secured and that an emergency evacuation of the aircraft remains possible.

Mass and balance requirements
(9) The pilot in command must ensure that during any phase of operation, the loading, the mass and, except for balloons, the centre of gravity position of the aircraft comply with any limitation specified in the flight manual, the weight schedule required by article 43, or equivalent document.

Fuel, oil and ballast
(10) The pilot in command must ensure that—
   (a) in the case of a flying machine or airship, sufficient fuel, oil and engine coolant (if required) are carried for the intended flight, and that a safe margin has been allowed for contingencies;
   (b) in the case of a public transport flight, the instructions in the operations manual relating to fuel, oil and engine coolant have been complied with; and
   (c) in the case of an airship or balloon, sufficient ballast is carried for the intended flight.

Performance based navigation
(11) The pilot in command must ensure that when performance based navigation is required for the route or procedure to be flown—
   (a) the relevant performance based navigation specification is stated in the flight manual or other document that has been approved by the CAA or another competent authority;
   (b) any navigational database required for performance based navigation is suitable and current; and
   (c) the aircraft is operated in conformity with the relevant navigation specification and limitations in the flight manual or other document mentioned in sub-paragraph (a).

Article 73

73 Passenger Briefings

(1) The pilot in command must ensure that before or, where appropriate, during the flight, passengers are given a briefing on emergency equipment and procedures.

(2) This article does not apply to the pilot in command of an aircraft registered in the United Kingdom in relation to a flight under and in accordance with the terms of a police air operator's certificate.

So, to comply with article 69 we must also ensure all documentation relating to our aircraft is in order.

Documents that should be checked for currency and correctness are: -

Certificate of Registration

Certificate of Airworthiness

Certificate of Approval of Radio Installation

Aircraft Radio Licence

Noise Certificate

Insurance Certificate

Certificate of Maintenance Review or Airworthiness Review Certificate

Certificate of Release to Service

Technical Log

This might seem a bit tedious and picky, but it is really just like any other pre-flight check. Remember that the C of A is only valid if all the relevant conditions are observed and complied with (e.g. a correct check 'A' being carried out). If the C of A becomes invalid for a flight then the insurance will too. Although aircraft do not have to be insured by law, you would rather foolhardy to fly without it. Most aircraft operators would ensure that all the above documents relating to their aircraft are in order and that the aircraft are operated correctly, but mistakes can happen and ultimately it is the pilot's responsibility. And sod's law would state the day you have your little dink with an aircraft, is the day there is a problem with the paperwork due to someone else's oversight!

Therefore, we can see that there are certain legal requirements to understand how our aircraft is equipped, operated and performs. However, hopefully in purchasing this booklet you are sufficiently self-motivated by interest or self-preservation to acquire a greater depth of knowledge of the aircraft you fly rather than to satisfy a regulation. If, at first, self-preservation is not a motivator then studying some of the accident reports provided by the AAIB may prove enlightening. Appreciating the limits of the aircraft's performance in differing circumstances and particular handling qualities will better equip the pilot to make the right decision in time of need. This may all seem a bit of "doom and gloom" and regulated but as pilots, when flying, we have a great duty of care to ourselves, our passengers and non-flyers below. That said, with knowledge rather than ignorance and hope, we can plan, prepare and take to the skies to enjoy our flying. End of lesson one!

The Piper Warrior

The Cherokee family of aircraft covers a wide range of variants from a 140hp two- seat version for the training market to perhaps the ultimate development in the Chilean ENAER T-35 Pillan military trainer. The T-35 being available in both piston and turboprop-powered versions! However, the basic range does include engine sizes from 150hp to the 200hp Arrow with retractable undercarriage and variable pitch propeller. So it is important to check, when hiring a Cherokee, which version you are about to fly as the performance can vary quite a bit. The advantage is that you can learn on a lower powered and normally cheaper aircraft and easily step up to a more powerful type with minimal differences training time.

The PA-28-151 Warrior was first introduced in 1974. It was a further development of the PA 28 Cherokee series that began in 1960 and had already seen a number of variants. With a completely new wing and powered by a 112- kW (150-hp) Lycoming 0-320-E3D engine the Warrior brought improved handling and performance. The interior was also improved both ergonomically and in the standardisation of the instrument panel. The latter was an important step towards a common flight instrument panel layout that was being used by all manufacturers. In 1977 the PA -28-161 Warrior II was introduced with a 119kW (160hp) Lycoming 0-320-D3G engine. Again further improvements in performance were achieved. At the same time a new 134kW (180hp) version, the original being first produced in 1962, named the PA-28-181 Archer II was introduced using a Lycoming 0-360-A4M engine. The Warrior II and Archer II are the most common variants to be found in the UK. The handling notes that follow relate to the Warrior II version although due to the commonality between later Cherokee models the main differences are in the performance achievable depending on the engine size. Where differences do occur these are noted in the text.

The Airframe

The Cherokee Warrior II is a semi-monocoque aluminium alloy construction. This means that the metal skin is riveted to an underlying structure of metal frames, longerons and stringers. A well-tried and tested construction method dating from the 1930's, it is sometimes referred to as a stressed skin construction as the metal covering "skin" does indeed form part of the load bearing quality of the complete structure. It is a conventional construction for a light aircraft of its period. Some fairing parts, and wing tips are made from GRP. The engine frame, made of tubular steel, is mounted to the foremost frame and firewall. The firewall is a thin sheet of metal covering the frame and designed to prevent, or at least delay, fire in the engine bay from entering the cabin. One of the major and certainly the most significant modifications from earlier models was the new semi-tapered wing. It replaced a rather basic design of parallel chord wing, giving much improved performance and also helps identify it from earlier examples. The new wing maintained the cantilever design, bolted to a central spar box that forms part of the fuselage. As the wing is mounted low on the fuselage lateral stability is provided by noticeable dihedral. Access to the cabin is through the only door fitted above the starboard wing, where the wing is strengthened and black walkway marked. It is important that only the area marked in black is stood upon otherwise damage may be caused to the wing. A step behind the flap is also provided to make access easier.

At the rear of the fuselage is a conventional fin and rudder assembly with a horizontal stabilator. Unlike a conventional fixed tailplane and separate elevator, in a stabilator type design the whole aerofoil section pivots to provide pitch control.

The Flight Control Systems

A Typical PA-28-161 Instrument Panel and Control Yokes

The Warrior is fitted with full dual controls for pilot training. The control wheel or yoke is used to operate the ailerons and elevators through a system of cables and pulleys. Although the cables pass over a number of pulleys in the system, the action felt when checking the aircraft on the ground before flight should be smooth and with little or no resistance. Anything untoward should be checked out further before flight.

Ailerons

Differential ailerons that can travel upwards through 25° and down by 12.5° are fitted to the outboard trailing edge of the wings. A mass balance, to prevent flutter, is attached by a small rod to the outer end of the aileron and concealed within the wing tip shroud.

Elevators

In the Cherokee series of aircraft the traditional tailplane and elevator has been replaced with a stabilator. Also known as an all-moving tailplane, as the complete horizontal surfaces move as one. It has freedom of movement upwards, from neutral, through 14° and down 2°. Because the whole surface moves, a very small or light control input would provide a very strong pitching force. This could over stress the airframe. To overcome this problem and provide the pilot with "feel" or some extra control column pressure an anti-balance tab is fitted. This can be seen extending right across the rear of the stabilator, with a linkage rod that controls its position, visible from below. Trimming of the stabilator is carried out in the normal way using a trim wheel mounted between the front seats that acts upon the anti-balance tab operating rod. This works in the natural sense, rotating the top of the wheel forward trims nose down and rearwards would trim nose up.

Rudder

The rudder is operated by the rudder pedals that are also directly linked to the steerable nose wheel, which can be moved 27° either side of straight ahead. Care is needed when taxiing to ensure that the pilot's feet are not protruding above the pedals, as the pedals are suspended from a torque tube mounted above the pedals and full deflection may be limited by ones' foot contacting this tube first.

Unusually for a light aircraft, the Warrior is fitted with a rudder trim that is controlled by a small wheel mounted centrally below the instrument panel. Rotating the wheel applies a spring pressure to the rudder linkage to relieve rudder pedal pressure. Clockwise rotation relieves right rudder pressure and anti-clockwise left rudder pressure.

Flaps

The flaps are manually operated through a lever between the seats resembling a rather large car hand brake lever and moved in a similar way by pushing in the button on the end. They are a simple slotted type that has three deployed positions, 10°, 25°, and 40° activated by a cable linkage. They are only fully locked when in the up position. In any other position they are prevented from coming up further than the position selected, but not down. A spring arrangement maintains the selected position, but not if someone steps on it! So beware when mounting the wing not to step on the flap unless it is secured in the up position. Occasionally this also becomes evident when checking an aircraft out if there is a wind blowing from behind the aircraft; in this situation after moving the control lever to raise the flaps they remain down! Confusing if you are not aware of the reason for this happening.

Engine

The first mark of Warrior (1974-1977) is fitted with a 150hp Lycoming 0-320-E3D engine rated at 2700 RPM. The later Warrior II (including the Cadet) has either a 160hp Lycoming 0-320-D3G or 0-320-D2A engine, again, rated at 2700 RPM. A more powerful engine of 180hp (0-360-A) is fitted to the Archer II, rated at the same RPM. This gives the Archer amongst other attributes a much better rate of climb and higher cruise speed for the same payload. Although this too is improved as we shall see later. The 320 and 360 in the engine designation refers to the cubic capacity in cubic inches, which equates to about 5.25ltr and 5.90ltr respectively. Compare that capacity and power output, to that of your average car of 2ltr producing something like 140hp and you will see that the engines, in common with most light aircraft, are relatively lightly loaded. With the large capacity comes a relatively slow revving engine, for a petrol engine, when compared to an automobile engine that freely revs up to 5 to 6000 or more. The engine is air-cooled using the popular four cylinder horizontally opposed layout. The picture below shows the engine as seen from above with some of the main components annotated. In common with most modern car engines a large proportion of the engine is made from aluminium alloys ensuring a good power to weight ratio. Unlike a modern car engine however, is the lack of sophisticated electronic engine management systems that might lead to glitchy electronic problems. A simple type of carburettor and a dual magneto ignition system ensure excellent reliability. The basic design of a large cylinder capacity, slow revving engine fitted with simple ancillaries is more akin to an old style tractor engine than any modern car engine!

Side View of Archer Engine

Rocker Covers

Heat Exchanger

LH Magneto

Electric Fuel Pump

Fuel Strainer Bowl

The Propeller

A two bladed, fixed pitch Sensenich 74DM6-0-60 or 74DM6-0-58 propeller is bolted directly onto the end of the engine crankshaft. The Warrior II and Cadet have a prop diameter of 74" and the Archer II 76". This gives an approximate ground clearance of ground clearance. During inspection the propeller is checked for damage to the leading edge, nicks and dents etc, and that tips are also undamaged. The propeller is a very sophisticated piece of equipment and even what might seem to be minor damage, can give serious problems if ignored. Poor taxiing technique or lack of observation whilst taxiing can easily lead to a prop strike on something like a taxiway light or even over rough ground. Also beware of carrying out power checks near loose stones or gravel. If a prop strike is suspected, then the engine must be shut down and a visual inspection carried out to assess damage.

The Engine Oil System

The oil system in an engine has to perform a number of quite arduous tasks that are not necessarily immediately apparent. As well as lubrication, oil aids cooling of internal components, removes by-products of combustion, provides corrosion protection and helps with the gas-tight sealing between the piston rings and the cylinder.

To achieve all these criteria the correct grade and type of oil must be used. Also the oil must be changed at the recommended interval time, as it gradually degrades in use and therefore, will not perform all of its duties correctly. Any engine manufacturer will lay down the specification of oil to be used in its engine and Lycoming are no different. Oil bought for a motorcar can vary massively in price for what may seem the same thing. The label of a cheap oil may state that it meets a particular required specification, and does so as it comes out of the can. Therefore, the purchase appears attractive. However, what it fails to mention is that the base oil of the product is of a low grade and will degrade far more quickly than a 'quality' oil. Hence, the sought-after protection etc for the engine will be compromised. An aviation grade oil ensures that the specification of the oil is still met after the oil has done its time working in the engine, maximising engine life. There are two oil specifications listed for the Warrior engine, depending upon whether the engine is within its first fifty hours of life or not.

First fifty hours   MIL-L-6080 Aviation Grade Straight Mineral Oil.
Thereafter   MIL-L-22851 Ashless Dispersant Oil.

The different types of oil must not be mixed. As with all things in aviation, if in doubt about the correct oil ask! Both types of oil are available in various viscosities to suit different average surface air temperatures.

In the POH Piper list the recommended oil viscosities for a particular range of surface air temperatures.

Example:
For a new engine or rebuilt components within first fifty hours.
Temp. -1°C(30°F) to +32°C(90°F)   SAE 40 MIL-L-6082 Straight Mineral Oil

After first fifty hours.
Temp. -1°C(30°F) to +32°C(90°F)   SAE 40 MIL-L-22851 Ashless Dispersant Oil

The SAE number shown reflects the viscosity of the oil. The lower the temperature the lower the viscosity should be. However, usually the oil container will have the commercial viscosity grade number printed on it, which is approximately double the SAE equivalent.

Therefore, the first example would have grade 80 Straight Mineral Oil. The second, being Ashless Dispersant Oil has a W prefix, therefore W80.

Bearing in mind the confusion that might arise in the oil department, it is advisable to check with the maintenance organisation responsible for your aircraft which type and grade of oil should be used in the engine.

A view of some of the oil system components in the Warrior.

Oil Pressure Pipe to Gauge

Oil Filter

Oil Filler and Dipstick

Engine Mounting Frame

The engines in the Warrior series have a wet sump (i.e. the oil reservoir is in the bottom of the crankcase). Oil is drawn from the sump through a gauze filter into the engine driven pump; this then pumps the oil under pressure to requisite parts of the engine. Firstly, though, the oil is directed to the oil filter where particle contaminants are removed. If the filter becomes blocked then a valve will open allowing unfiltered oil to bypass it and continue round the system. This is only likely in the event of the filter not being changed at the correct service period. After the filter, the oil flows to the oil cooler, mounted at the back of the engine.

The oil cooler can be seen here at the back of the engine on the left.

Oil Cooler Matrix

A thermostatic by-pass valve allows cold oil to by-pass the cooler, which helps the oil warm up more quickly on start up when the oil is cold. From here the oil is fed past a pressure relief valve and on to the oil galleries within the engine crankcase that supply all the various moving parts within the engine. The relief valve works by directing any over pressure oil back to the sump, bypassing the moving bits. One reason for ensuring the oil is at a reasonable working temperature before take-off, is that it is easier for the pump to generate over pressure oil with cold oil. This means that a reduced volume of oil is reaching the important parts of our rapidly revolving engine, when, more than ever, we wish the engine to carry out its task to the best of its ability! This is one good reason for having the oil temperature gauge that is fitted. A pressure gauge is also fitted and mounted alongside the temperature gauge on the instrument panel. Although, in common with most engines, this is only measuring the pressure at one point in the engine and with cold oil especially this may be quite different at another point. An oil pressure warning light is incorporated in an annunciator panel (in addition to a vacuum and alternator warning light) in most of the Warriors and Archers that illuminates if the pressure drops below 35psi. An adjacent button is used to test the function of the warning lights when the engine is running.

Oil capacity: 8US quarts

A couple of further points worthy of mention are: Firstly, following checking of the dipstick for volume, take care when replacing the dipstick not to over tighten the cap (especially when the engine is hot), as it may prove very difficult to undo. Secondly, as the oil drains back to the sump by gravity, it takes a while before an accurate reading as to the volume in the sump can be made, if the engine has been running.

A Typical Oil System

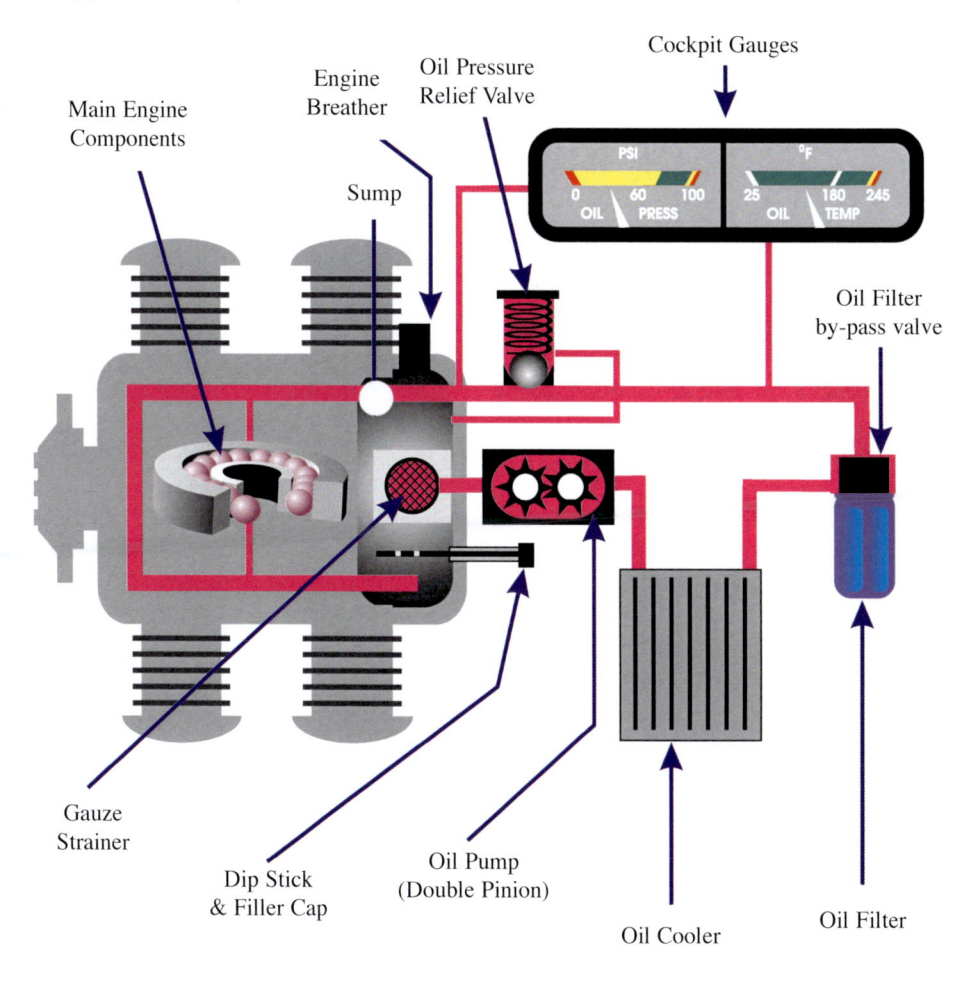

The Fuel System

Normal fuel used is Avgas 100LL (coloured blue)
Also approved: 100 (formerly 100/130) (green)

The fuel is stored in two aluminium wings tanks, installed into the leading edge of each wing with a filler cap on top and a drain valve underneath the wing. A vent pipe also protrudes beneath each wing tank to allow air to replace the fuel as it is drawn from the tank. Each tank is connected to the fuel selector valve located on the lower left hand cabin wall, just in front of the seat. A pipe then leads through the firewall to connect the selector valve to the fuel strainer bowl mounted on the lower left of the firewall. Externally a drain valve for the strainer bowl is accessible through a small hole in the engine cowling. There are two fuel pumps fitted to the Warrior, an engine driven pump and an electric one; each are fed by a fuel pipe from the fuel strainer. The pumps supply pressurised fuel to the carburettor, and this pressure can be monitored on the fuel pressure gauge in the cabin. An engine primer system is also fitted that feeds three of the cylinders and draws fuel from the fuel strainer bowl. The primer is a simple piston and cylinder type pump and is mounted adjacent to the throttle quadrant on the instrument panel. A peg and locking collar is fitted to prevent inadvertent action. Turning the operating knob to line up the peg (on the piston rod) with the slot in the collar will allow the pump knob to be pulled out. This fills the pump with fuel, which, when pushed back in will deliver the fuel directly into the cylinder head near the inlet valve. Normally 3 or 4 strokes are sufficient to aid starting but this does vary between types and also the ambient and engine temperature. When not being used for starting purposes the primer must be locked to prevent fuel being drawn through the system. This would cause an over rich mixture and rough running of the engine.

A Schematic Diagram of the Fuel System

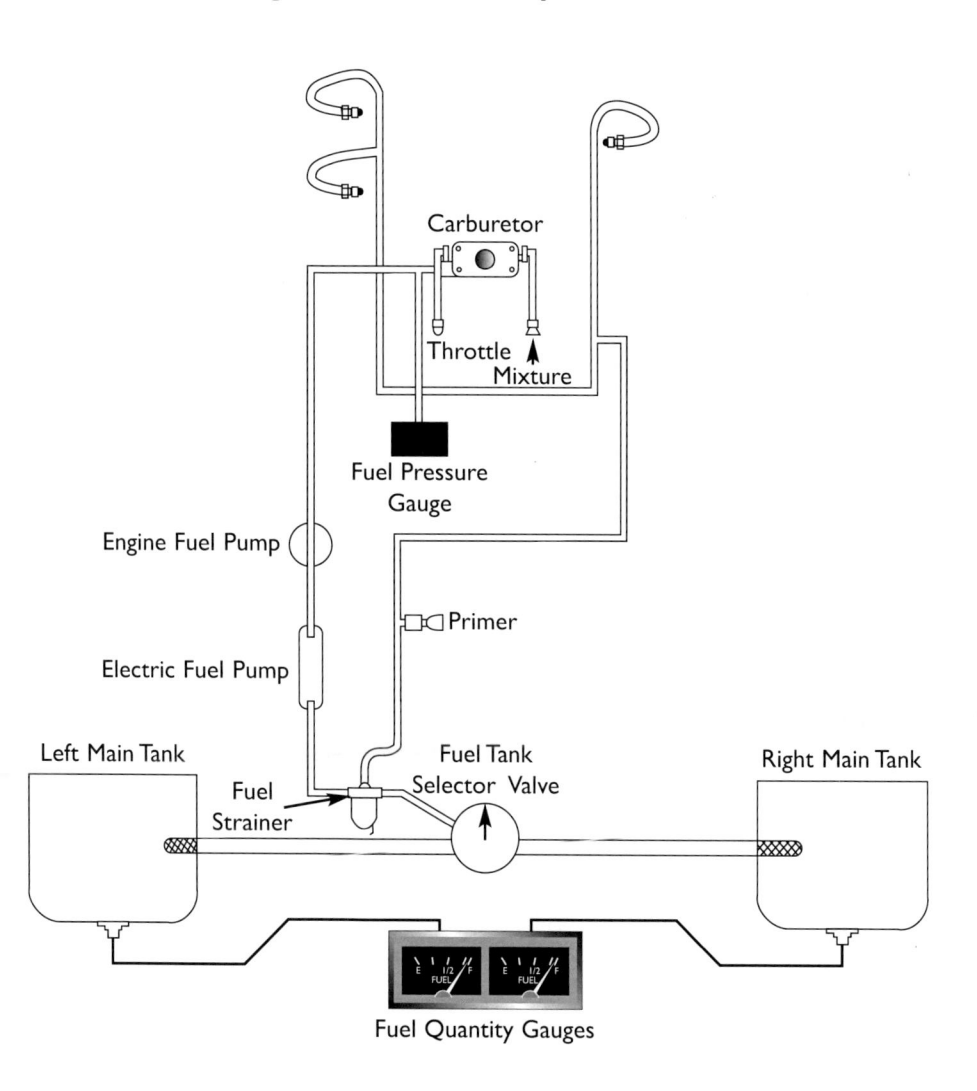

Fuel Tank Capacity:

	US Galls	Litres
Total	50	189.3
Unusable	2	7.6
Usable	48	181.7

The fuel tank filler neck has a metal tab that protrudes down into the tank to show a fuel level of 17 US gals/64.35ltr per tank. This gives a total of 34 US gals/128.7ltrs, which is useful when the passenger payload prevents taking max fuel due to weight restrictions.

Each tank has a fuel drain to sample the fuel for contamination, as does the fuel strainer bowl, which is a water and sediment trap prior to the fuel reaching the carburettor. When using the fuel drains for the checking of the fuel, care should exercised to ensure that the drain has properly closed after use as it is possible for it to remain open. This may happen for two reasons, one the basic design of the drain that originally had a small lip on it, to secure the valve in the open position, which would assist the draining of the tanks. Helpful if you are an engineer removing fuel from a tank, but not if you are a pilot requiring the fuel to keep the engine running!

Secondly, the drain valve is closed by being spring loaded, and it is possible for bits of dirt to prevent the closing action from being totally successful. So always check after using the drains, that fuel does not continue to flow from the valve. Also when checking the strainer bowl drain the fuel selector valve should be on, otherwise it would be possible to miss the fact that this drain was still open after checking the fuel. You are also unlikely to be able to drain much fuel off unless one of the tanks has been selected on the fuel tank selector valve.

Fuel Strainer Bowl Drain

Fuel Strainer Bowl with Cowling Removed

- Fuel feed to Carb
- Fuel feed to primer
- Fuel supply from tanks
- Drain Valve

Fuel Tank Selector Valve

- Spring loaded off lock

The fuel selector can be awkward to operate if you are flying the aircraft from the right hand seat (as an instructor would). In that case anyone occupying the left hand seat should be briefed in the correct operation of the valve before a flight. By virtue of its position in the cabin it is also out of view and care needs to be taken in the correct operation and of fuel management. Out of sight can lead to out of mind. So ended one sorry flight from my home airfield a couple of years ago to an unfortunate pilot who did not change tanks during a relatively short local jolly. On final approach with about two miles to go the engine gave up running on fumes, being deprived of the perfectly good fuel in the other tank, the aircraft landed somewhat short of the airfield much to the disapproval of the undercarriage! Of the occupants, luckily, only pride was dented, the aircraft was rather more affected. The selector cannot be moved to the off position without first depressing the spring loaded safety catch detailed in the photo above. This is virtually a two handed operation and prevents the off position being accidentally selected but not the case of running out of fuel on one tank whilst there is plenty in the other!

As mentioned earlier there is a mechanically driven pump and an electric pump to get the fuel from the tanks to the carburettor. The electric pump is really a backup unit should the engine driven pump fail. It is therefore normally only used during take off and landing and when changing tanks.

Fuel System Components

The position of the engine gauges varies slightly between the Warrior and Archer, but in the picture below we see a Warrior set up of gauges.

The Carburettor

It is very, and sometimes vitally, important to know how the carburettor and its controls function to get the best and safest performance from the engine. A carburettor is based on a simple principle, yet can end up as a very complicated piece of engineering. However, the pilot can still benefit from understanding how a basic carburettor works.

In the following diagram we can see a cross-sectional view of a simple carburettor similar to the type fitted to a Piper Warrior.

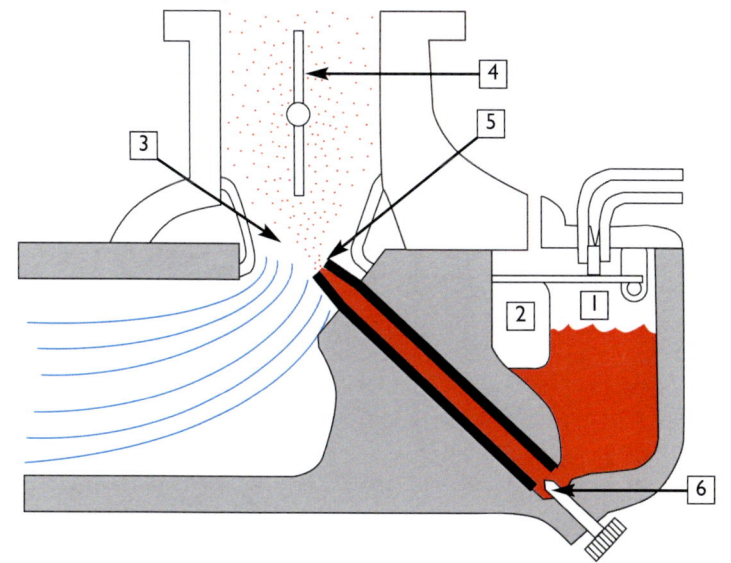

Fuel is fed from the strainer to the float chamber (1) of the carburettor. This is basically a small reservoir and the float (2) controls the fuel level by acting on the needle valve above. Basically a toilet cistern in miniature! In the body of the carburettor holes or drillings are formed to allow the passage of fuel to various parts of the carburettor.

Air is fed to the carburettor by way of ducting to a central passage called the venturi (3). It is here that the mixing of fuel and air takes place. The air valve (4), or more commonly called butterfly valve, is connected via linkage to the lever type throttle on the instrument panel. This valve controls the amount of fuel/air mixture going to the engine by changing the volume of air that passes through the venturi. For the most part, fuel enters the venturi via the main jet (5) due to the low pressure caused by the venturi effect. When the throttle is in the idle position, it is virtually closed and there is insufficient airflow to draw fuel through the main jet. However, a low enough pressure is developed adjacent to the idle jet (not shown) to draw a reduced fuel flow through this jet. Fuel to both jets has to pass through the mixture control valve (6). This valve is connected to the red mixture control knob, mounted adjacent to the throttle, and is used to directly control the amount of fuel going into the fuel/air mixture. This control is also used to shut off the fuel supply to stop the engine. Stopping the engine this way attempts to ensure no unburnt fuel is left in the intake tract of the engine, thus helping to prevent accidental starting should the propeller be inadvertently moved.

The mixture control can be used in two ways: Firstly, to stop the engine by pulling the lever back and down to the fully lean position that cuts off the fuel supply to the engine. Secondly, it can be moved towards the lean position until a particular fuel ratio is achieved. This is discussed further later and termed leaning.

Finally, the carburettor fitted to the Warrior is also fitted with an accelerator pump and jet. This is also linked to the throttle, so that whenever the throttle is moved forward an additional amount of fuel is pumped into the airflow to combine with that from the action of the venturi. This ensures smooth acceleration of the engine when the throttle is opened. Although, there are a couple of points to note with this type of carb. Firstly, rapid opening the throttle to full can cause too much fuel (for the quantity of air) entering the engine and causing a rich cut. In this type of engine, this just means it will probably cough and hesitate for a few seconds before picking up to full revs. However, on much larger piston engines like some of those that powered the military aircraft of thirties and forties it could have a more serious effect. One tragically sad example of this happened to a restored Bristol Blenheim. After many years in the rebuild, the aircraft crashed in its first season following a low approach and go around to an airstrip. Unfortunately the pilot was unaware of the devastating effect opening the throttles too quickly would have on the mighty Bristol engines. With large accelerator pumps delivering masses of fuel, the engines effectively quit and the aircraft came to a very messy end on the ground. Luckily, although the aircraft was damaged beyond repair, those on board escaped serious injury. Another example of "know your aircraft"! Getting back to our Warrior, we should also appreciate that when starting the engine pumping the throttle and priming is likely to deliver more fuel than is necessary. This runs the risk of flooding the engine, leading to possible poor starting and increased fire risk. As aircraft can be notoriously individual when it comes to starting procedures, please check you are using a preferred sequence on your aircraft.

The Carburettor and other Components

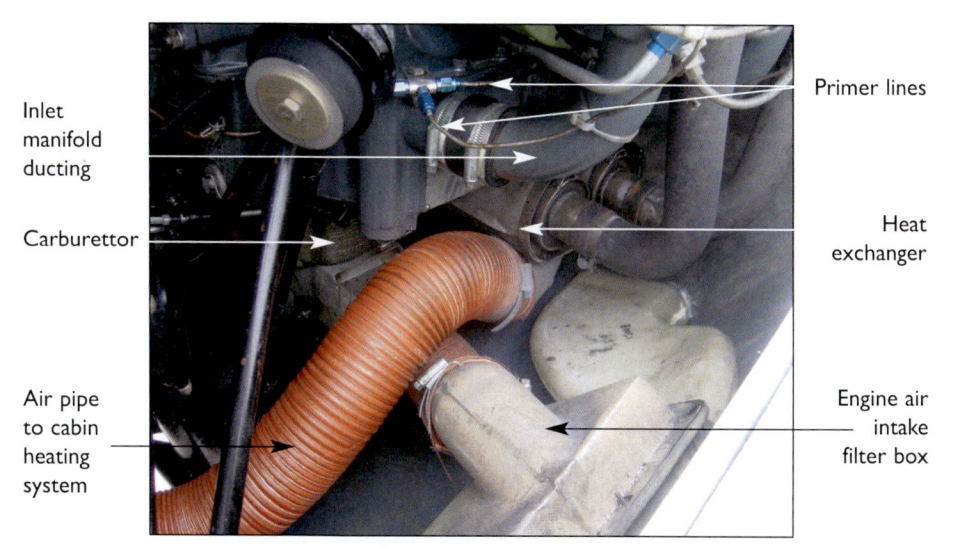

Inlet manifold ducting

Carburettor

Air pipe to cabin heating system

Primer lines

Heat exchanger

Engine air intake filter box

Carburettor and Carb Heat Valve

Carburettor body

Warm air intake

Normal air intake

Carb heat flap valve

Fuel is fed to the carburettor from the fuel strainer mounted on the firewall. Air is ducted to the carburettor air box from either the front mounted intake and filter, or a heat exchanger around the exhaust pipework (an unfiltered source). Within the carburettor air box is a simple valve that is operated by the carburettor heat control knob mounted on the instrument panel. Use of this is covered later.

The carburettor fitted to the Warrior is known as an updraft type, as the air is fed into the bottom and drawn through to the top. The mixture then passes up through a tube in the sump that (when warm) serves a dual purpose. Firstly, the mixture is warmed slightly, which aids fuel vaporisation and secondly assists in oil cooling due to this heat transfer. Past this point the inlet manifold branches out to supply each cylinder with mixture through the inlet port and valve.

The Engine Controls

Primer

RPM gauge

Carb heat control (cold position)

Mixture control (lean position)

Throttle (idle position)

The Throttle

As mentioned before, this controls the amount of fuel/air mixture reaching the engine that in turn controls the speed/power of the engine. Rotational speed of the engine is displayed on the R.P.M. gauge mounted on the left of the throttle quadrant. Normal idle speed is about 500-700rpm and maximum 2700rpm with a red line on the gauge to show this limit.

Maximum rpm obtained at full throttle will depend upon the engine load and airspeed. So, whilst you cannot "red line" the engine if stationary on the ground, it is quite possible to do so in the air. A lever to adjust the friction is provided so that it is possible to lock the throttle or adjust its resistance to movement.

The Mixture Control

This is used to adjust the ratio of the fuel/air mixture for optimum engine performance. The exact procedure should be set out in the POH in a Lycoming supplement. There are various methods that can be used to achieve a desired fuel/air ratio depending on the instrumentation fitted to the aircraft. A complex type aircraft may have a fuel flow gauge, exhaust gas temperature (EGT) or cylinder head temperature gauge. However, none of these are fitted as standard to the Warrior, although an EGT gauge may be fitted on the Archer. So, often all we have to work with is the RPM indicator when adjusting the mixture and to some extent the airspeed.

The Leaning Procedure

Basic Rules:

Always observe red-line temperature limits during take-off, climb and high performance cruise power operation. Whenever mixture is adjusted, rich or lean, it should be done slowly. Always return mixture to full rich before increasing power setting. At all times, caution must be taken not to shock cool the cylinders.

Set the throttle to give the RPM that will produce the power required at the cruising altitude currently being flown (this information is obtained from the engine performance graphs in the POH, a sample of which is reproduced in the performance section). Next, slowly move the mixture control lever towards the lean position to reduce the fuel flow in the carburettor. Depending upon how over rich the mixture is, the RPM will slowly increase by a small amount and then start to reduce. At the maximum indicated RPM or maximum airspeed, achieved by this method, the maximum power mixture will have been achieved. This is slightly different from the best economy mixture, which would deliver the best range and endurance figures. It should also be noted that at the best power mixture the airspeed would also be slightly higher. Information on both best power and best economy mixtures for cruising are available in the POH in graphical format. To achieve the best economy mixture, which gives the most miles per litre of fuel, the leaning is continued, slowly, until engine operation becomes rough or engine power rapidly diminishes as noted by an undesirable decrease in airspeed! When either condition occurs, enrich the mixture sufficiently to obtain an evenly firing engine or regain most of the lost airspeed or engine RPM. Some engine power and airspeed must be sacrificed to gain a best economy mixture setting. The reduction in RPM from best power to best economy is typically 25 - 50. Any further leaning of the mixture would be a false economy and would eventually lead to serious engine damage. It would also cause the engine to lose significant power and run roughly, surely focusing the pilot's attention on the error! If the engine does not run smoothly or a sharp drop off in rpm is observed, as a guide, en-richen the mixture slightly as necessary to restore smooth running. Care will be needed when leaning the mixture to prevent over doing it. Therefore, this might be best practised on the ground first so that you are familiarised with the procedure needed to achieve the performance desired. Moreover, spark plug fouling can be a problem with some aircraft engine designs and using a correctly leaned mixture can reduce this. Although we use the term "leaning the mixture", what we are actually doing is reducing an over rich mixture to the correct ratio. In the good old days, if you had a car with a manual choke, for instance a Morris Minor, and had driven the said car around with the choke out, which enriches the mixture, it would not be long before the old bus would start coughing and behaving like you were trying to run it on some kind of dodgy old moonshine!

Without getting too technical, the internal combustion engine runs most efficiently with a mixture of about 1 part fuel = to 15 parts air (by weight) known as a 1:15 ratio mixture. The average aircraft carburettor is set up to give a ratio of about 1:12 at sea level as a basic setting. Efficiency aside, this aids engine starting and cooling. It also reduces the likelihood of pre-ignition and detonation, both of which are undesirable. As well as efficiency, the fuel/air ratio also affects the amount of power the engine can develop at any given rpm. Starting to sound complicated?! Well, now we will go and fly our aircraft to an altitude where the density of the air is much less than at sea level and complicate matters even more! In the performance section of the POH graphs display information on fuel consumption figures for various stages of flight.

Sample Engine Performance Graph

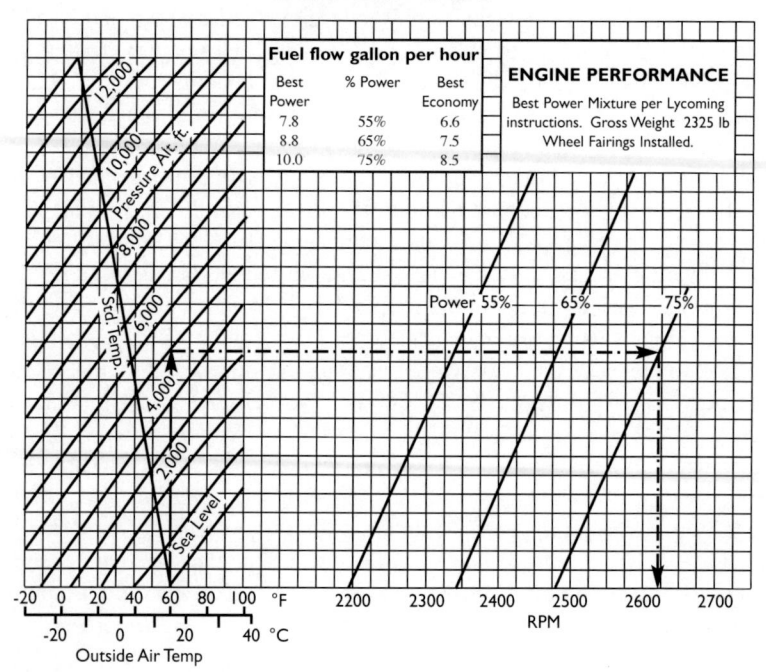

PA-28-161

Fuel flow gallon per hour		
Best Power	% Power	Best Economy
7.8	55%	6.6
8.8	65%	7.5
10.0	75%	8.5

ENGINE PERFORMANCE
Best Power Mixture per Lycoming instructions. Gross Weight 2325 lb Wheel Fairings Installed.

If we study the graph we can see how much power the engine is delivering at a given rpm, altitude and temperature. Although some of the differences may not seem too great, the significant differences are between the various % power figures and their related fuel consumption values. Applying this information to a typical cruise using the typical 2300rpm setting. It can be seen that setting a higher than planned rpm, say 2550, can produce a significantly higher fuel consumption. Conversely, if was required to stay airborne for longer than originally planned, a lower rpm of 2200 will reduce the fuel consumption. Therefore, when planning a flight ensure that you as the pilot are managing the engine to achieve the fuel consumption you expect! When to lean? Almost any time is the short answer. It is recommended when cruising at any altitude and using 75% or less power. It is permissible to lean for max rpm (i.e. max power) in the climb above 3000ft and will definitely be useful above 5000ft. However for most local and short navigation flights leaning could be left until established in the cruise phase.

As mentioned previously an over lean mixture is undesirable, due to the reduced cooling provided by the mixture and the onset of detonation, which will destroy the engine. With this in mind any change in operating conditions (i.e. power setting or altitude) will require a resetting of the mixture control.

For maximum service life it is recommended that during continuous cruise an engine power of 65% or less is used and the cylinder head temperature is maintained at 400°F or below, with the oil temperature remaining between 165°F and 220°F. However, the Warrior is not normally fitted with a cylinder head temperature gauge so this might prove difficult to monitor!

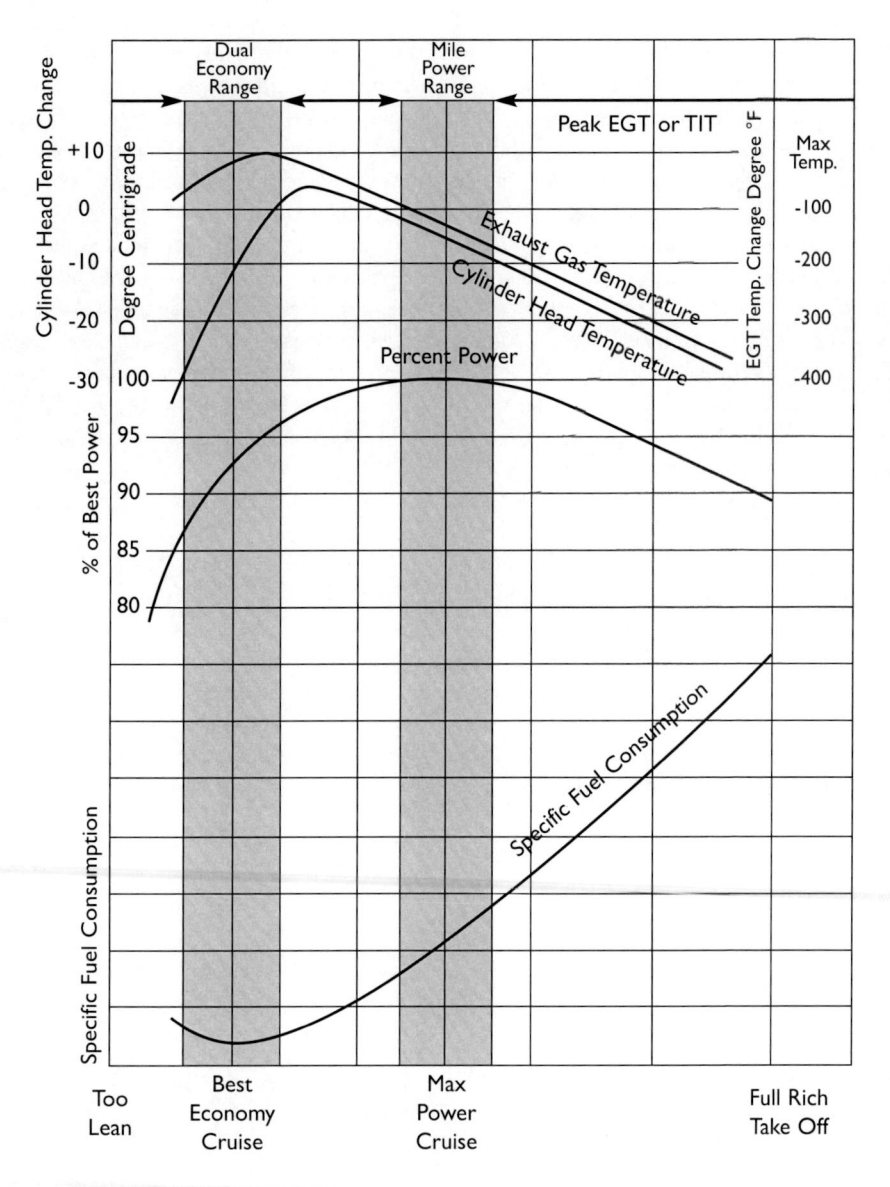

This representative diagram show the effect of leaning on: Cylinder Head Temperature, Exhaust Gas Temperature or Tit, Engine Power and specific Fuel Consumption for a Constant Engine RPM and Manifold Pressure.

Note: Textron lycoming does not recommend operating on the lean side of Peak EGT.

Carburettor Heat Control

To facilitate the removal and prevention of carburettor ice, a system that can supply warm air to the carburettor is fitted. A heat exchanger that is wrapped around the exhaust system is connected via a simple flap valve to the carburettor intake. The valve is operated by the carburettor heat control mounted on the right of the throttle quadrant.

It would be very easy to misunderstand carburettor ice, its formation and the actions required to prevent and clear ice accretion. So it is important to understand the basic physics going on inside the throat of a carburettor venturi. Without getting too technical, as air passes through the venturi it speeds up, cools down and the local static air pressure decreases. The decrease in pressure provides the suction (fundamental to the function of a carburettor) to draw the fuel from the float chamber through the passages and into the airflow via the appropriate fuel jet. A jet is a very fine hole that regulates fuel flow. However, the downside of this process is that the cooling effect of the airflow is increased by the fuel evaporation, absorbing latent heat from the surroundings. So the inside of a carburettor venturi can become very cold, freezing in fact, even though the outside temperature is quite warm. And if the humidity is high enough, we have a recipe for carburettor ice to form. As the venturi is already a fairly small place, it might not take long for enough ice to form, sufficient to restrict the venturi by an engine-stopping amount and turn your powered aircraft into a glider! Ice tends to build up on any protrusions or bends where the air contacts a surface at sub zero temperature and can occur on the ground as well as in flight. We need to be on our guard for carburettor ice at any time, as it could really spoil your day if not spotted soon enough! One fallacy is to believe it needs to be cold or visible water needs to be present for ice to form in the carburettor. Obviously, to form ice, water is required and it is available in plentiful supply in vapour form in moist air masses; like those that usually cover most of the UK. Even in summer! Indeed warm air can support more water vapour than cold. As relative humidity is a measure of the water content of the air, this is a very useful guide as to how wet or dry the air is on a particular day. We know the temperature drop within the carburettor can be considerable (up to 30°C) and water freezes at 0°C and below. So, this combined knowledge helps us gauge the likely risk of carburettor icing on a given day. A very useful chart that elaborates on this phenomenon is produced by the CAA and is reproduced below. It can be seen that the ambient temperature does not have to be zero or 100% relative humidity for the risk of carburettor icing to be high. If not already familiar with the subject then further useful information can be found in AIC 145/1997 (Pink 161). As the ice forms in the carburettor it restricts the fuel air mixture rather like closing the throttle would. So, the first symptom in the Warrior is a gradual loss of engine RPM. This may initially be overcome by an increase in the throttle setting, if not noticed as carburettor (carb) icing. Further icing would cause a further drop in engine rpm, leading to rough running and eventually engine failure. However, good engine management would encourage the pilot to operate the carb heat control on a regular basis. If ice is present in the carb, one of two reactions is likely on application of the carb heat. Either, the engine will start to cough a little as the ice is melted and water passes through the engine with an associated large drop in rpm. Or, the rpm will almost immediately start to increase. Neither of these is the normal response to checking the carb heat system, therefore they warn the pilot of carb ice and that conditions are conducive to carb icing. With the foregoing in mind it is obvious that the carb heat control is an important engine management tool and explains why it should be checked carefully on the ground before flight. However, its use on the ground should be limited, because when selected, it supplies the engine with an unfiltered source of air that could pass damaging airborne contaminants (dust, grit etc), which will increase engine wear. Also, using hot air to supply an engine operating at 75%hp or more is not recommended as detonation may occur, causing serious engine damage. Therefore always ensure that the carb heat is off when selecting full power. Using a source of hot air to run the engine also reduces the amount of power the engine can develop as it reduces its efficiency, as warm air is less dense than cold air.

The carb heat control should be thought of as a switch, either on (hot air) or off (cold air) and no in-between setting. To check its function, a note of the current rpm should be made, then select hot air (carb heat knob pulled out fully) for about 10 seconds. Note the small drop in rpm (50 -100) then reselect cold air (carb heat lever up). The rpm should return to the original value, if however it returns to a higher value, then carb ice was present.

In the section discussing the mixture control we saw how it varied the fuel/air ratio; in selecting carb heat we also affect this ratio. The warm air supplied by the carb heat system, being less dense, causes an increase in the richness of the mixture. For the temporary nature of a carb heat check this is not a problem. However, if for some reason it was decided to fly with the hot air selected constantly on then the mixture control may have to be adjusted for best engine performance. During a descent when the carb heat is normally selected for the duration this is not an issue, as the mixture needs to be enriched anyway, and the overriding factor is the prevention of ice in the carb. It is also important that the carb heat is selected before reducing power to clear any ice prior to descent and check that it is still working correctly.

Extract from AIC P077/2009

3   Atmospheric Conditions

3.1   Carburettor icing is not confined to cold weather and will occur in warm weather if the humidity is high enough, especially when the throttle butterfly is only partially open as it is at low power settings. Flight tests have produced serious icing at descent-power with the ambient (not surface) temperature above 30° C, even with a relative humidity as low as 30%. At cruise power, icing can occur at 20° C with a relative humidity of 60% or more. Ice accretion is less on cold, dry winter days than on warm, humid summer days because the water vapour content of the air is lower. Thus, where high relative humidity and ambient temperatures of between -10° C and +25° C are common, as is the case in the UK and Europe, pilots must be constantly alert to the possibility of icing and should take the necessary steps to prevent it. If the appropriate preventive action has not been taken in time it is vital to be able to recognise the symptoms (see paragraph 4.2) so that corrective action can be taken before an irretrievable situation develops. Should the engine stop due to icing it may not re-start or, even if it does, the delay may result in a critical situation.

3.2   Carburettor or fuel icing may occur even in clear air and these are, therefore, the most insidious of the various types of icing because of the lack of visual clues. The risk of all forms of induction system icing is higher in cloud than in clear air but because of the visual clues the pilot is less likely to be taken unawares.

3.3   Specific warnings of induction system icing are not included in standard weather forecasts for aviation. Pilots must use their knowledge and experience to estimate the likelihood of its occurrence from the weather information available. When information on the dewpoint is not available, pilots in the UK and Europe should always assume a high relative humidity, particularly when:

(a)   the surface and low-level visibility is poor, especially in the early morning and later evening and particularly when near a large area of water;

(b)   the ground is wet (even with dew) and the wind is light;

(c)   just below the cloud base or between cloud banks or layers;

(d)   in precipitation, especially if it is persistent;

(e)   in cloud or fog - these consist of water droplets and therefore the relative humidity should be assumed to be 100%; or f in clear air where cloud or fog has just dispersed.

3.4   The chart below shows the wide range of ambient conditions conducive to the formation of induction system icing for a typical light aircraft piston engine. Particular note should be taken of the much greater risk of serious icing with descent power. The closer the temperature and dew-point readings, the greater the relative humidity.

CARBURETTOR ICING IN AIR FREE OF CLOUD, FOG OR PRECIPITATION
(risk and rate of icing will be greater when operating in cloud, fog and precipitation)

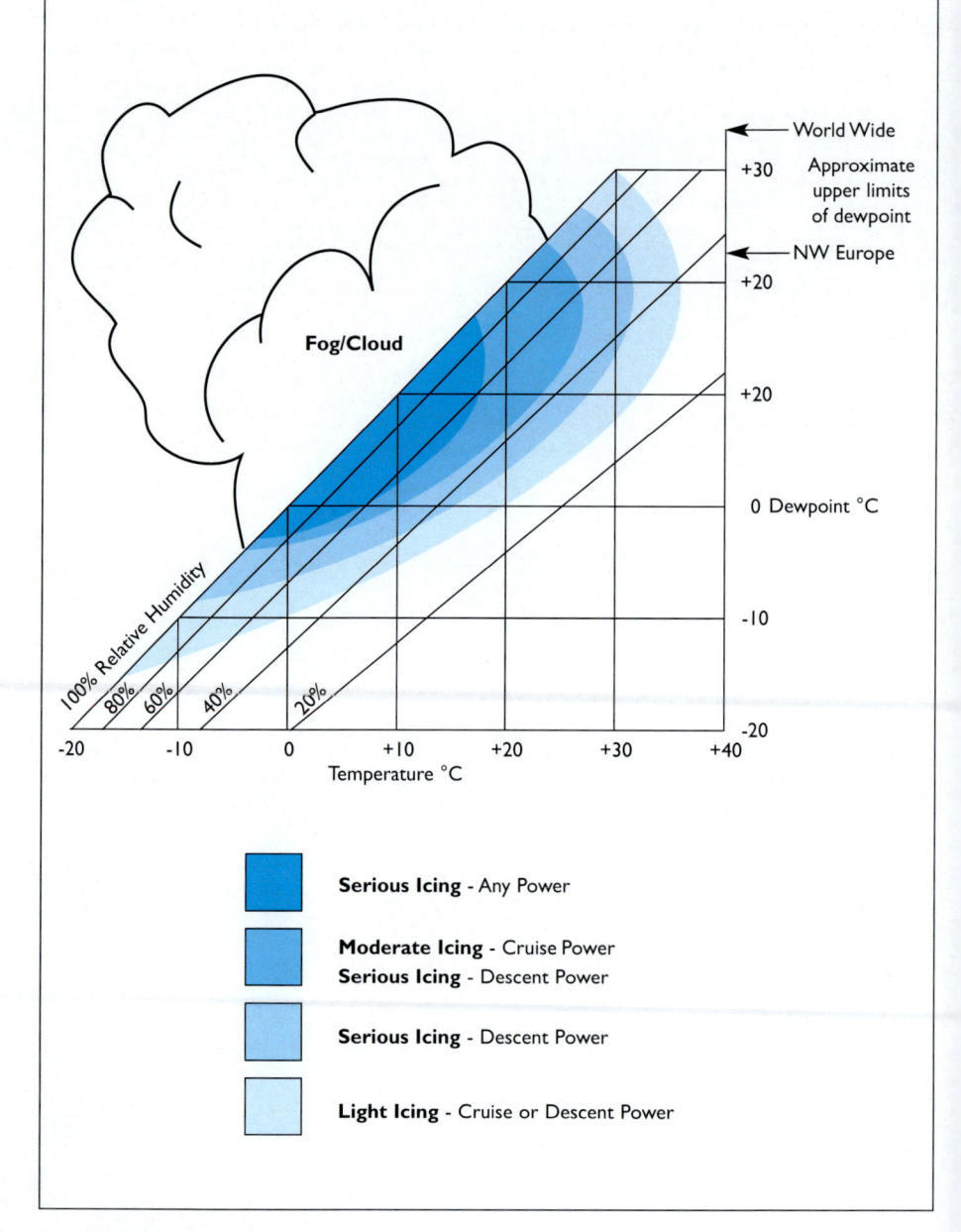

Serious Icing - Any Power

Moderate Icing - Cruise Power
Serious Icing - Descent Power

Serious Icing - Descent Power

Light Icing - Cruise or Descent Power

The Ignition System

The engine is fitted with a dual magneto ignition system. Two spark plugs are fitted in each cylinder and two magnetos mounted on the rear of the crankcase. High voltage capacity (also known as high tension) leads join the two components. There are two reasons for a dual ignition system. One, safety, should one system fail, secondly, due to the relatively large bore of the engine, a better, more efficient fuel burn is achieved. The magnetos are termed left and right due to their respective positions on the engine. The magnetos are not connected to the rest of the electrical system and do not require any external electrical power source to function. A magneto uses the property of a moving magnetic field inducing an electric current in an adjacent coil of wire. In a magneto the magnetic field is rotated whenever the engine crankshaft is rotated, with the potential to generate a spark (at the spark plug) unless the primary (low voltage) circuit of the system is shorted out.

Due to the rotation of the magnetic field, an electric current is induced in the primary coils of the magneto which itself gives rise to another magnetic field around the coil so long as the circuit is complete. Also in the primary coil circuit is a set of contact breakers (that are controlled by the relative position of the crankshaft and magneto) and the mag switches. Considering only one cylinder, when the piston is at the correct position to receive a spark from the spark plug in order to fire, the contact breaker points open. This causes the magnetic field that has been created by the induced electric current in the primary coil to spontaneously collapse. With me so far, because it is a bit like the chicken and egg story! Additionally there is a secondary set of coils in the magneto assembly that have many more turns of wire than the primary coil. When the primary field collapses so spectacularly it induces a voltage in the secondary coil that by its nature will generate a voltage of many thousands of volts, enough to jump the gap in the electrodes of a spark plug. It is this voltage therefore that fires the mixture in the cylinder. This is then repeated for all the cylinders. The timing of the spark is crucial and this is controlled by a cam acting on the contact breaker. If the contact breaker is shorted out of the circuit then the primary coil magnetic field cannot collapse and no spark will be generated. This is what the magneto switches do. A glance at the wiring diagram below of a simplified typical magneto circuit shows the magneto switch in the on position which conventionally would be off, as in this condition it breaks the circuit. A reversal of what might be expected. Therefore, this shows the circuit in the live condition, to make it safe the magneto switch is closed which shorts out the action of the circuit breaker and therefore prevents a spark occurring at the spark plug. Therefore the system is only safe when the primary circuit is short-circuited. So, if the switch fails or a wire becomes disconnected or broken then this would not be possible and the system would remain live. However, this has the advantage that it would not affect the ability of the engine to run. Hence, the respect and reason for always treating a propeller as live.

Simplified Typical Magneto Wiring Diagram

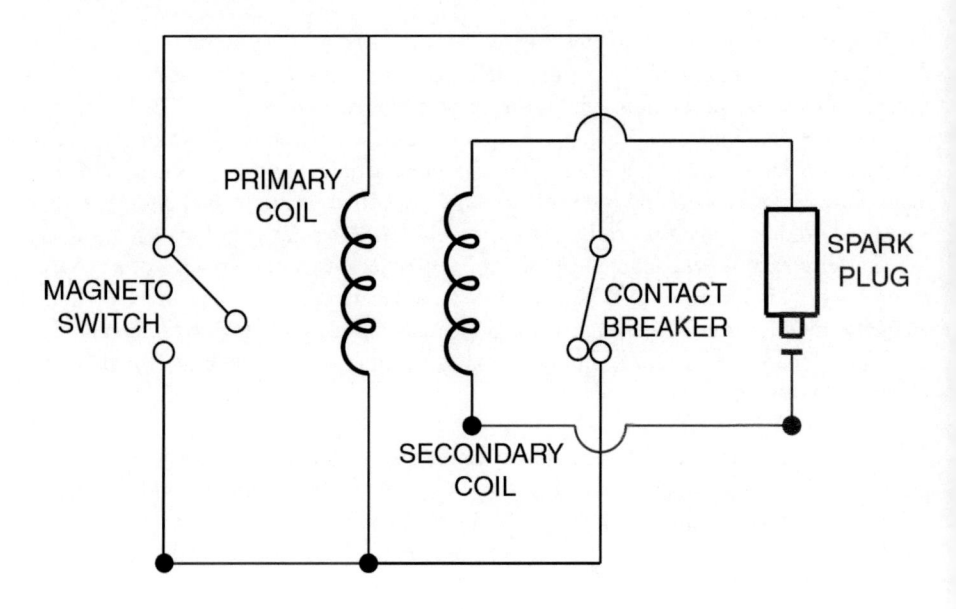

The blue link wires would normally be connections made through the frame of the aircraft called earthing, which reduces actual wiring.

The contact breaker remains in the closed position until opened by the action of crankshaft driven cam when a spark is required in one of the cylinders.

A four-position magneto switch is used to start the engine with positions of off, right, left and both. The start position is spring loaded to return to the both position and in most cases requires a push in and turning action to engage the starter motor. Hand starting is possible but not recommended. If doing so then the "left" magneto should be selected, which has an impulse coupling fitted to aid starting and reduce the possibility of kick back. Once started, the magneto switch should be turn to the "both" position.

The Electrical System

Terminology used in this section that may require explanation.

Relay or Contactor: Electro-magnetic switch. A small wire coil is energised to produce a magnetic field capable of operating a switch very quickly with heavy electrical contacts. This enables a small electrical current to control an electrical circuit using a much larger current (e.g. a starter motor circuit). One advantage is the saving of weight by using shorter heavy cable runs.

Alternator: Electrical generating device capable of producing power even at low rpm. It produces alternating current that is passed through a rectifier/voltage regulator control unit converting it to direct current that can then be used in charging a battery and/or driving D.C. systems.

Bus: An electrical link, which connects the circuit breakers to a common supply path.

Magneto: An assembly of fixed permanent magnets and wire coils on a spindle that when rotated generates a high voltage electrical current, used to power the spark plugs of an engine. Needs no external electrical power source to function.

Starter Motor: An electric motor requiring a very large current to produce sufficient torque to turn the engine over. It is only designed to operate for short intervals of time, otherwise it will overheat and burn out! When energised it engages automatically with a gear bolted to the crankshaft.

Circuit Breaker: An electrical device that will heat up when an electrical current in excess of the rated value is passed through it, causing a bimetal strip to open a pair of contacts, thus interrupting the current flow and consequently switching off the circuit. Generally these types of devices have replaced fuses in electrical circuits, as they are more convenient.

Electrical Power Supply

The Warrior is fitted with a 14 Volt dc electrical system, powered by a 60 amp alternator and 12 volt battery.

The battery is fitted inside a thermoplastic box and mounted either underneath the rear right side passenger seat or on the front of the firewall on the right. In the Archer the battery is mounted behind the baggage compartment rear panel.

The alternator, which powers all the electrical services once the engine is running, is mounted on the front of the engine and driven through a V belt, (which, although not easy, should be checked before flight). Its electrical output is fed to a regulator unit mounted behind the instrument panel on the left before entering the rest of the system. The electrical system is energised through the master switch, which is the left most switch of the row of electrical rocker switches. It is a dual-rocker type switch, which means the battery and alternator can be separately switched.

The battery side is switched on to check the electrical equipment on the ground before engine start and the alternator side operated after start. Or, the switch may be operated as one. Without the engine running and the master switch on, the battery will supply the power to ground check the electric services. Beware though of the limited capacity of the battery, if overused it may not be possible to start the engine, especially if the battery is not in the best of condition or if it is a very cold day. A further point to note is that an alternator requires a small voltage before it will start supplying any electrical power, when rotated, called excitation. Therefore, if the battery is flat and the prop hand swung the to start the engine you may find that the alternator will not give any output.

To aid starting with a low battery Warriors are fitted with an external power supply socket. This is located on the right-hand side of the fuselage just behind the luggage compartment door. Before using this ensure the external power source is of the correct voltage (i.e. 12 Volts) and the master switch is off before connection.

To use this facility, use the following procedure:

- Check master switch and all electrical services are off.
- Ensure external power source is the correct voltage (some are dual voltage) and polarity.
  Insert the external power source plug into the aircraft socket.
- Turn on the master switch and start as normal.
- After engine start, turn off the master switch and all electrical services.
- Remove external power source plug from aircraft socket.
- Turn master switch back on and check ammeter indication. It should show reasonable load (battery charging). If no output is displayed then do not fly, the battery will need to be removed for charging or replacement before flight.

The picture below illustrates a typical switch layout.

As we can see, after a number of years' service the labels on these switches have almost faded to the point of invisibility! However the re-labelling above the switches clarifies the situation. The anti-collision light switch is sometimes also a dual rocker switch, controlling wing tip strobes and rotating red tail fin light. The panel lights are switched on using the right hand rotary switch, which also controls the illumination level for night flying. The left hand rotary switch is used to switch on the navigation lights and control the illumination level of the radio lights.

Simplified Electrical Circuit Diagram

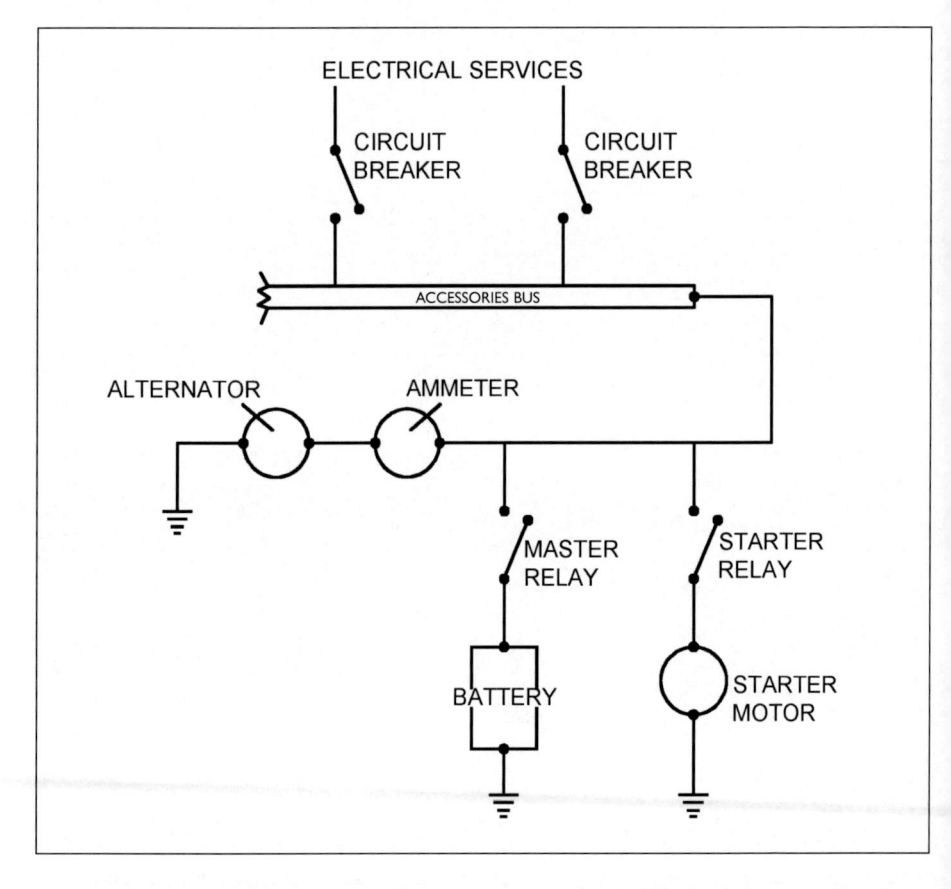

If the electrical circuit diagram is studied we can see that all electrical equipment is connected via circuit breakers to a common line or bus. Before the alternator is generating power the battery supplies all the electrical power to the bus. When the alternator is generating power it takes over the job of supplying power to the bus, via the ammeter, and also charges the battery. An ammeter is fitted into the circuit between the alternator and the bus, it displays the total load on the alternator. So, as more electrical services are switched on the total current drawn from the alternator, and displayed on the ammeter, increases. In normal circumstances it will show a small charge going to the battery after start to indicate a battery in good condition being topped up following the drain put on it by the starter motor. As well as an ammeter, an alternator warning light is fitted in the row of annunciator lights that is tested with the press to test button.

Electrical Power Consumption

It is a good idea to have some concept of the amount of electrical power the different systems on the aircraft consume. We can get an indication of this by the size of circuit breaker fitted to the circuit. Furthermore, if an item is not fitted with a switch it will be a very low consumer of power. For example the fuel gauges. At the other end of the scale, anything involving the generation of heat (such as a pitot heater) will be a large consumer of power. A motor also requires a large current and the starter motor the most current of all. Lights come somewhere between the two extremes with, not surprisingly, the brighter the light the more power it requires. Therefore, if an alternator failure is suspected (this is covered in more detail later) then the electrical load on the battery can be minimised by not using the high consumers especially, unless necessary.

Starting at bottom end of power consumption, the fuel gauges (one for each tank) are located with the other engine monitoring gauges and are powered by floating level sensors in the fuel tanks. As the float position varies with the amount of fuel so does the amount of power fed to the gauge. Beware that this is a very archaic system and very prone to inaccurate readings on the fuel gauges and any pre-flight check must include a visual check of the fuel tank contents. Compared to the system and information displayed in a modern car it is quite prehistoric! However, the same could be said of all aircraft of similar vintage design. Adjacent to the fuel gauges are the oil temperature and pressure gauges. Of these two the temperature gauge is electrical, receiving a signal from a sensor fitted into an oil gallery in the engine.

There is also a low oil pressure warning light mounted in the pilot's field of view on the instrument panel, powered by an electrical sensor in an oil pressure line feeding the gauge. This warning light together with an alternator failure light and low vacuum light make up a small annunciator panel, with a test button to the left to check the bulbs. All the lights should illuminate when the button is depressed.

The Annunciator Panel

The Turn Co-ordinator is also electrically operated with a motorised gyro and therefore unaffected by a suction failure that would render the Attitude and Direction indicators unserviceable (u/s). The normal lighting on the Warrior is to have navigation lights in each wing tip and tail, a rotating beacon on the tail and/or strobe lights in the wing tips and a landing/taxi light. The strobe lights and rotating beacon may be operated by a single rocker switch or a split dual rocker switch. The split switch enables them to be selected separately. Of all the lights, the landing light would consume the most power and they also have a habit of burning out easily. Therefore they should be switched off when not required.

The two remaining switches control the pitot heat and the electric fuel pump. As mentioned before, the pitot heat is a high consumer of power, which incidentally is at risk of burning out if left on too long whilst the aircraft is stationary on the ground. The electric fuel pump is normally only used during take off and landing and when changing fuel tanks. It provides a backup should the main pump fail. An electric fan may be fitted to assist with ventilation, with the control switch mounted next to the normal cabin heater controls on the lower right of the instrument panel. A real luxury for the UK would be to have the optional air conditioning fitted. When in use this not only consumes electrical power but significant engine power and must be turned off for take off and landing. Although available option, it is only likely to be found on an Archer or the more powerful Arrow.

The Starter Motor

A starter motor is fitted to the front lower left of the engine crankcase, the front end of which can be seen through the opening in the cowling. The ring gear that is bolted to the crankshaft can also be seen. When the starter key switch is operated, the starter motor rotates and the drive cog on the motor shaft is propelled along the shaft to engage with the ring gear, which then turns the engine. When the engine starts and the key released, power is disconnected from the starter motor and the drive cog should disengage and return to its original position. If it does not, then the engine will be rotating the starter motor. If this happens, as the engine rpm increases the starter motor could disintegrate in a rather alarming fashion! Also the motor will become a generator and could produce a potentially very damaging unregulated electrical power supply. Hence the reason for fitting a warning light for this condition. This is checked after start to show if the starter motor is still engaged.

A Typical Starter Motor Circuit

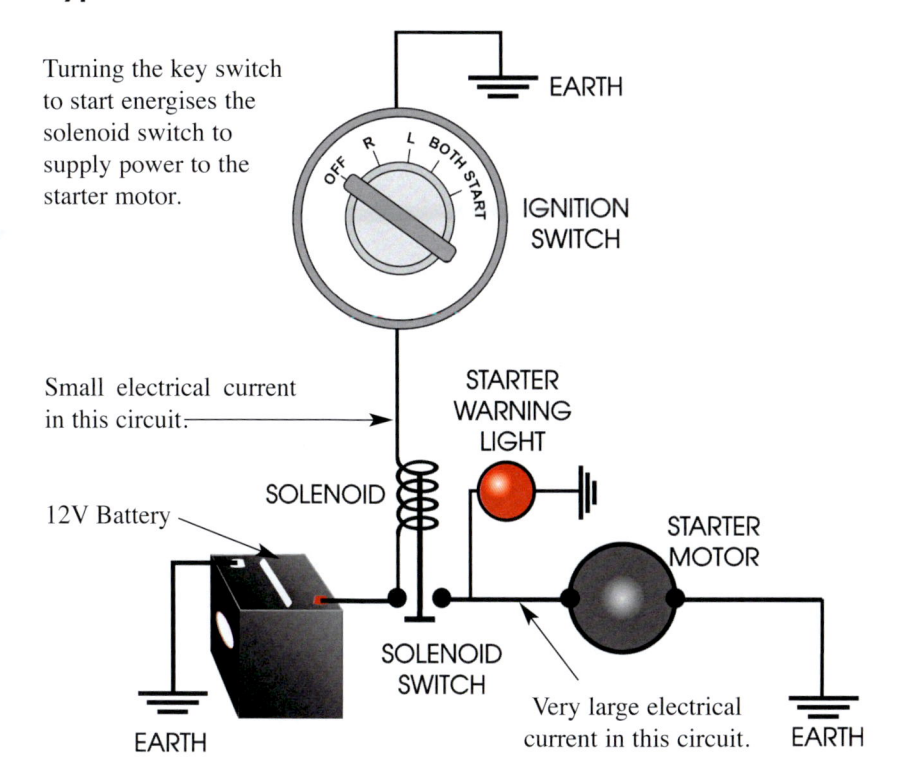

Turning the key switch to start energises the solenoid switch to supply power to the starter motor.

EARTH

IGNITION SWITCH

Small electrical current in this circuit.

STARTER WARNING LIGHT

SOLENOID

12V Battery

STARTER MOTOR

SOLENOID SWITCH

Very large electrical current in this circuit.

EARTH

EARTH

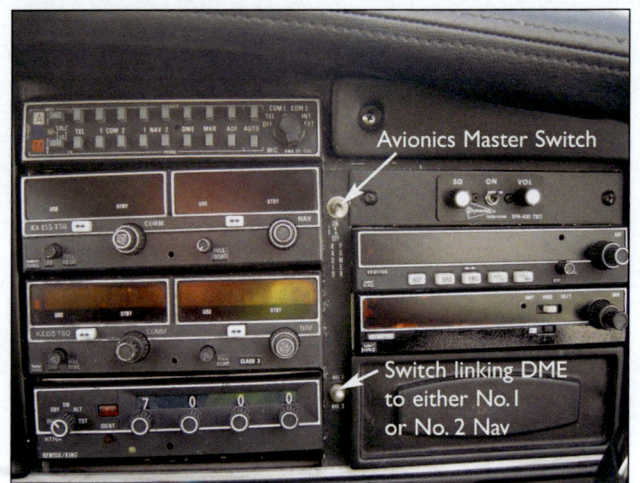

Avionics

The only remaining electrical consumers are the avionics or "Radio stack" which can vary enormously. Due to the longevity of the Warrior series radios range between the old clunk click variety to a modern all singing all dancing type requiring a small mortgage to purchase. Illustrated below is a middle-of-the-road set up, with two digital flip-flop combined navigation/communication radios complemented with a transponder, ADF and DME equipment.

Typical Avionics Installation

A control panel resides at the top of the stack that enables switching between the various radios and the cabin loudspeaker or headset system. On the left of the panel is a marker beacon facility and the far right the transmitter selection switch. In between, are two rows of buttons that are used to select which radio is listened to and whether headset or loudspeaker is used. This also allows more than one station to be monitored at any one time. The far right of these buttons are the auto selectors that automatically link the radio receiver output to that of the transmitter frequency selected on the communication (Com) transmitter (Tx) switch.

Loudspeaker Selector Buttons

On/Off Switch also selects com Tx

Headset Selector Buttons

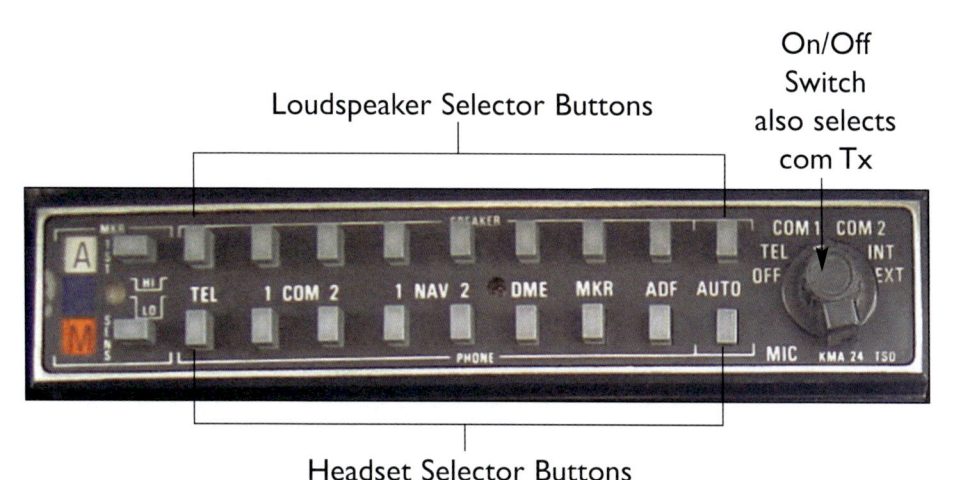

With the Com/Tx switch positioned at Com 1 (as above) and the auto button depressed on the lower bank, then the station frequency tuned on the number one Nav/Com will be heard through the headset and transmitted to when the transmit button is pressed. If the com two button on the lower bank is also operated, then the station tuned on the number two Nav/Com will be heard through the headset too. To transmit to the number two station the com/Tx switch has to be moved to the Com 2 position. To listen to any of the navigation stations tuned for their identification signal the appropriate selector button is depressed and volume set on the radio equipment. On the radio stack illustrated above there is a master avionics switch that enables all the avionic equipment to be switched off with a single switch. Another toggle switch is provided to link the DME equipment remotely to either of the Nav radios. As there are many different types of radio installations fitted to the Warrior it is an important point to familiarise yourself with the operation of all the radio equipment in your aircraft before flight. This will help prevent what might appear to be a radio failure, when in actual fact a switch or button is not in the correct position!

The Stall Warner

A metal tab protruding through a square hole in the leading edge of the port wing is connected to a switch mounted within. When the angle of attack of the wing approaches the stall the airflow moves the tab upwards and the switch activates a warning horn in the cabin. This occurs at about 5 - 10 knots above the stall.

Electrical System Malfunctions

The alternator is protected from electrical overload and over-voltage. Overload is controlled by the alternator circuit breaker. Over-voltage is controlled by an automatic control unit that monitors the system voltage and switches off the alternator should more than about 16volts occur in the system. This helps to protect the voltage sensitive electronics in the rather expensive radios etc. If this were to occur, then the ammeter would display a zero reading, as the battery would be supplying all the electrical power. Depending on the electrical load at the time, the low voltage light will also illuminate. However, it is possible that the condition was caused by a transitional peak in voltage and that the system would otherwise function correctly. It is possible to reset the automatic over-voltage unit by switching off the alternator side of the master switch for a couple of seconds and then back on again. If the reset has worked then the ammeter should show a normal reading and the low voltage light extinguish. If, however, the ammeter still displays a zero reading and the low voltage light is on, then the alternator has failed and a landing as soon as practicable should be considered. With the battery supplying all the electrical power it will last about 30 minutes with minimal load. It would be prudent to reduce the electrical load to the minimum required for safe flight.

As explained before, the magneto system, which supplies the engine with electrical power to run, is completely separate from the normal electrical system. So any electrical system failure will not affect the ability of the engine to operate, allowing the pilot time to assess the probable cause. As we have seen, the individual systems are protected by circuit breakers that pop out if their load limit is exceeded. It is possible to try and reset these, but only once and only after a short period of time to allow them to cool down, say a couple of minutes. However, if the tripped circuit breaker was accompanied by an acrid smell of burning plastic I would be rather suspicious that there was some form of short circuit that could lead to a fire and definitely not try to reset the breaker. But take some more immediate action to ventilate the cabin, identify the circuit concerned and its importance to the continuation of the flight. By cutting off the electrical power to the faulty circuit, the tripped circuit breaker has done its job, preventing the problem from getting worse. It is then up to the pilot to decide on the subsequent best course of action.

The Vacuum System

The attitude and direction indicators are air-driven gyroscopic instruments, powered by the vacuum system. An engine driven vacuum pump provides a vacuum regulated to 5.0 +/- .1"hg below the ambient pressure and a gauge mounted on the right of the instrument panel displays this. A relief valve/regulator is fitted to maintain the vacuum at the correct level and a reading outside the desired range implies a system malfunction. The pump is driven via a soft shareable drive coupling to prevent further problems should the pump seize. Should this occur the vacuum gauge reading would drop to zero. Air entering the system passes through an air filter to prevent damaging airborne particles reaching the instruments. If the filter does become clogged or blocked, a low reading would result as air enters the system through the regulator bypassing the instruments and gauge.

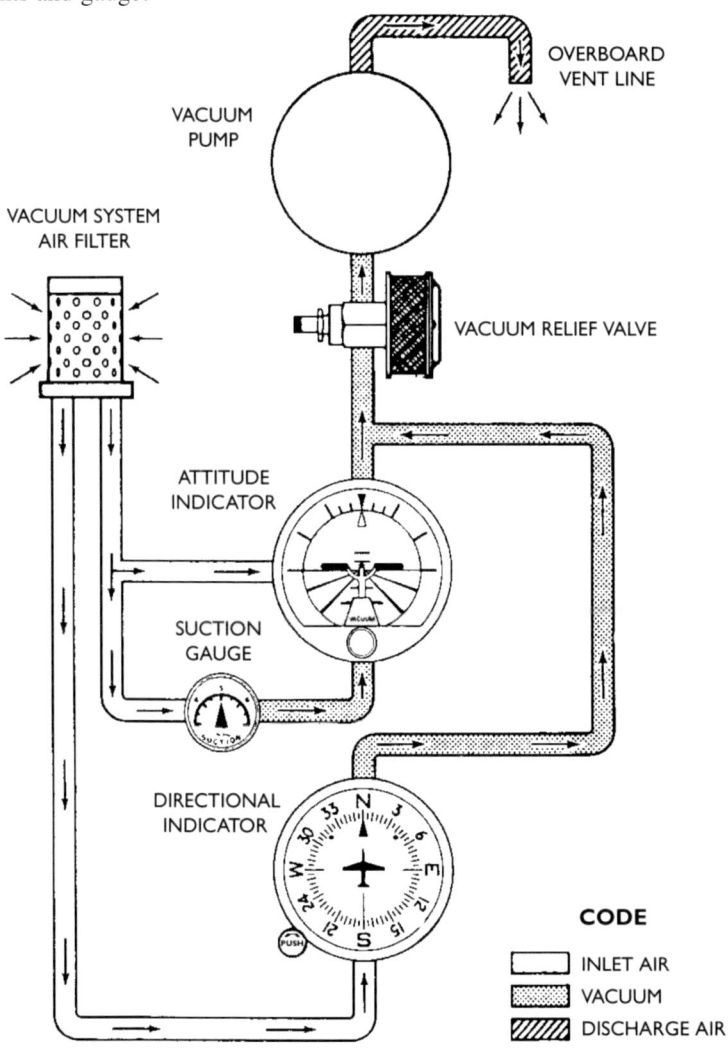

Some aircraft are fitted with an electrically operated auxiliary vacuum system. This system is intended for in-flight backup only. The system will consume about 15amps of electrical power so all unnecessary electrical equipment should be turned off before turning on the auxiliary system.

The Undercarriage and Braking System

The Warrior is fitted with conventional fixed tricycle undercarriage. Suspension is provided on all three wheels by oil and air oleo struts. On the ground, pressurised air within the strut supports the weight of the aircraft and provides a spring action to absorb landing and taxiing loads. When the strut extends or contracts, oil is forced through a restriction thus providing a damping action for the air spring. To ensure that the correct amount of spring action is available the oleos are checked for the amount of chrome piston tube visible when parked. The nose leg oleo should display about 80mm (3.1/4") and the main gear about 115mm (4.1/2"). This will vary slightly depending upon the load in the aircraft at the time. However, if insufficient extension appears visible then the strut will have to be re-pressurised as it may fail to provide sufficient suspension action during landing, unless it is a particularly good greaser! If it is the nose strut, taxiing may also prove to be troublesome as the strut could bottom out reducing propeller ground clearance. If oil appears to have leaked out of the strut during inspection, then the damping action it provides will be reduced. This could also allow the strut to bottom out on landing and during taxiing; this could become evident in banging noises coming from the offending strut.

Wheel fairings are factory fitted to the Warrior but in service many have had these removed. This follows experience operating from wet grass strips, where mud is thrown up into the fairing where it builds up to form a particularly good brake! Not a lot of benefit during take off! During cruise flight the wheel fairings improve the airspeed by a couple of knots, so not having them fitted is no great loss. The main wheels are fitted with 6.00 x 6 tyres and the nose wheel a 5.00 x 5 tyre (Archer 6.00 x 6).

The rudder pedals are directly linked to the nose wheel for steering through 30° either side of straight ahead (20° on the Cadet). A spring centring device is fitted to the nose wheel linkage, which also doubles as the adjustable rudder trim. As a consequence of the direct linkage the rudder can only easily be checked for full and free movement whilst taxiing.

Park Brake Lever and Rudder Trim Wheel

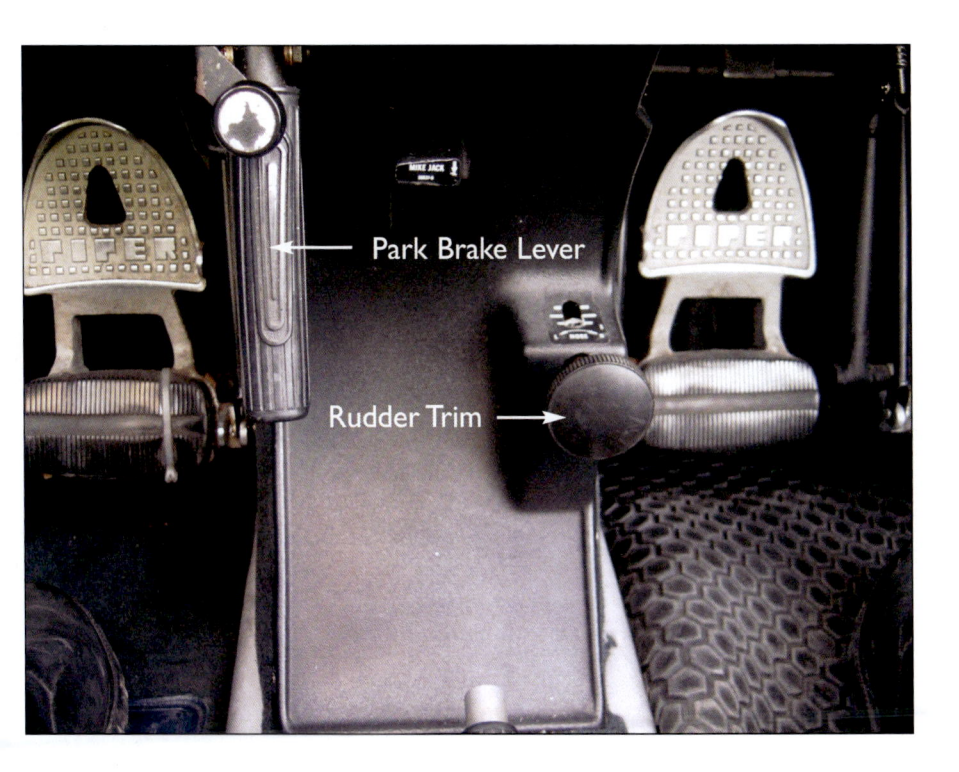

Park Brake Lever

Rudder Trim

The nose leg oleo is fitted to the engine frame that in turn is bolted to the firewall bulkhead. Although this is good at absorbing the shocks from undulations on the ground whilst taxiing, a heavy landing on the nose wheel is a completely different matter. This would completely compress the oleo and pass the impact shock to the engine mounting. Deformation can then easily occur in the oleo itself and/or the engine mounting and possibly the bulkhead. And for good measure the propeller will probably chew up the runway. Not the desired outcome of a nice flight! It is therefore imperative that the initial landing load be absorbed by the main wheels that were designed to take it. AAIB reports such as like the following, feature regularly in the monthly bulletins.

Aircraft – Piper PA28 - 180

After a local area flight the pilot returned to the airfield to carry out a series of touch and go landings on grass runway 26. The weather conditions were fair with a surface wind of 230∞/10kt. The first approach was flown at 80mph with full flap, and the pilot was content with the speed and angle of approach. He flared the aircraft slightly late however, and it touched down on three points. He attempted to control the subsequent bounce, but on the second touchdown the aircraft bounced again. The pilot commented that he was over-controlling the aircraft by this stage and was established in a series of pilot induced oscillations. A third, more severe, bounce followed resulting in the aircraft touching down hard in a nose down attitude. This damaged the nose landing gear and the firewall and caused the propeller to strike the ground. The aircraft eventually came to rest and the pilot, who was uninjured, was then able to vacate it without difficulty.

Something went wrong for which the aircraft was not designed and this wasn't a training incident, which are more prevalent. However, when reading reports of accidents such as this don't be too judgemental on the unfortunate pilot without considering what your actions, in the same circumstance, would have been. If a similar thing were to happen to you there is very little thinking time, only reaction time. Would your reactions be correct?

Hydraulic disc brakes are fitted to each of the main wheels. A hand lever mounted centrally below the instrument panel is used to operate the brakes, with a side catch provided to enable it to act as a park brake. Pulling the lever backwards, towards the pilot, applies even pressure to both brakes and operating the catch will lock the lever in the desired position for parking. Pulling on the lever again automatically releases the locking catch allowing the lever to move forward to the brakes off position. However, most Warriors are additionally fitted with toe brakes operated by applying pressure to the tops of the rudder pedals. Using the toe brakes enables differential braking (i.e. independent left or right braking) to be used, which improves the ability to turn the aircraft in small spaces. However, being too enthusiastic with the pedal pressure could lock the brake completely and cause the tyre to scrub across the ground leading to possible damage. Each toe brake (and they may be on both sets of rudder pedals) and the hand brake has its own master cylinder, fed with brake fluid from a reservoir mounted on the front left of the firewall. This may be checked for the correct amount of fluid, on those aircraft with lift up engine cowlings, as illustrated on page 48.

Brake Fluid Reservoir (PA 28 - 161)

Main Wheel and Brake Assembly

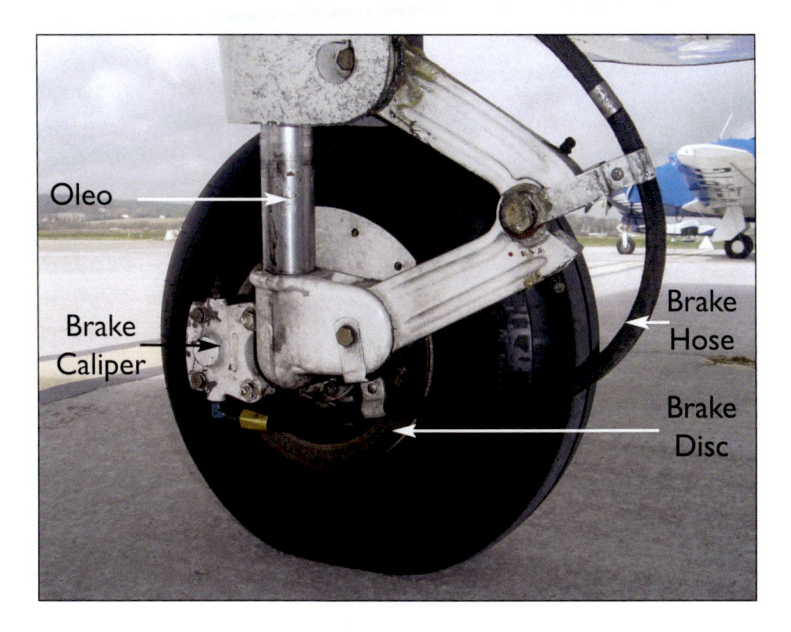

The Pitot Static System

The altimeter, airspeed indicator and vertical speed indicator are all connected to the pitot static system. On the Warrior the pitot head and static vent are combined in a single unit, called the pressure head, mounted under the left wing.

Combined Pitot/Static Head

The pressure head is fitted with an electric heater element that is used to prevent or clear blockage from ice. Remember the proviso that the **PA28 is not cleared for flight in known icing conditions.** However, it may inadvertently occur so ensure that the heater is working on the ground before flight. The vents themselves should be carefully checked. All sorts of bugs adore small holes in which to lay eggs and nest, which would block the free passage of air and hence cause the instruments to malfunction. If something is found blocking a vent, then an engineer will probably be required to dismantle the vent completely to remove the offending article. Do not blow into the vent in order to dislodge the blockage, as this would probably make matters worse and may well damage the instruments.

Diagram showing Pitot Static System

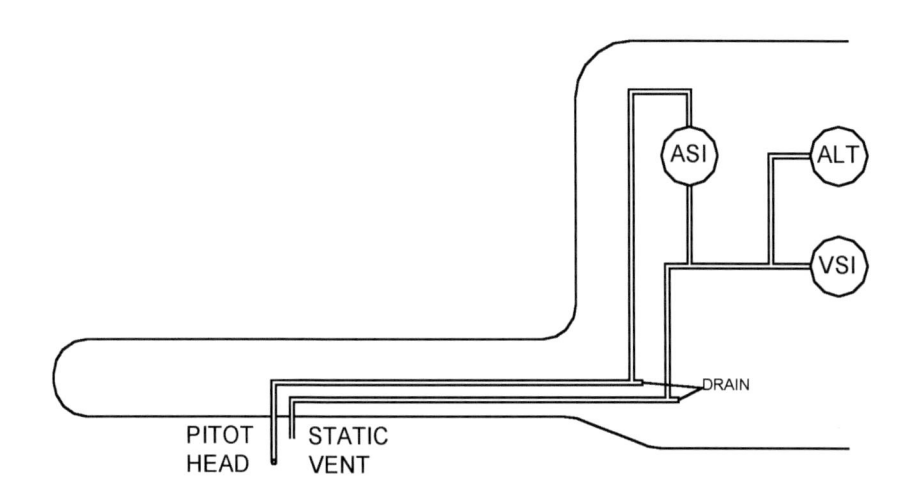

As we can see in the diagram above the pitot static system is responsible for the information displayed on the ASI, Altimeter and VSI. Although all the instruments fitted to the aircraft are there for a reason and most useful for accurate flight, failures are possible but it does not mean we can't continue safely if already airborne. Not that one would want to continue longer than necessary, but application of basic "power plus attitude equals performance" flying techniques enables the aircraft to be flown quite successfully and this should never be forgotten. However, whereas there is very little we can do about a blocked pitot in flight, the Warrior is fitted with an alternate static supply should we suspect a problem due to erroneous readings on the instruments. The switch to select alternate static is mounted under the left side of the instrument panel and should be checked before flight to be in the correct position. Herein lies the importance of checking that the airspeed indicator appears to be functioning correctly during the take off roll and if not, abandoning the take off. When did you last practise flying without a fully working airspeed indicator? This should be done under the guidance of a flying instructor, maybe on your next dual flight check! I mention this with the thought of a recent fatal accident where the only thing wrong with the aeroplane was the airspeed indicator. As this is not a flight training manual it is not the place to go into detail about instrument errors that occur when either a static or pitot vent is blocked. So if you are unsure about this then it may be time to check the subject out. If the alternate static source is being used then the readings will differ slightly from the true values and the cabin vents and DV window should be closed; whilst the heater and defroster should be turned on. Drain valves for the pitot and static lines are installed at the lowest part of the system on the lower left cabin wall and should be operated before flight to drain out any moisture.

The Pitot and Static Drain Valves

The compass is mounted centrally just above the instrument coaming and an outside air temperature gauge higher up in the left hand windscreen.

Outside Air Temperature Gauge and Compass

Heating and Ventilation

A heat exchanger mounted around the exhaust pipes supplies warm air via a control flap to the cabin area. The warm air can be directed to defrost the windscreen and/or to the vents on the floor between the front seats. The control levers for operating the control flap and directing the warm air are mounted on the lower right of the instrument panel. This functions quite effectively once the exhaust pipes are hot, which takes very little time. Although there is no blower facility on the warm air system the air blast from the propeller pushes the air through the system, which is improved when actually flying. However, we do have to bear in mind that the source of the warm air is from around the exhaust system. In a normally perfectly sound system there is no problem, but should a crack or fracture of some sort develop in the exhaust system, then potentially fatal gases could be directed into the cabin. The danger comes from the Carbon Dioxide (CO) present in the exhaust fumes. Being odourless, colourless and tasteless CO is not easy to detect and a pilot should be familiar with its effect on the human body. Often CO detectors in the form of a small disc of material that reacts to the presence of CO are fitted in the cabin. But these should not be relied upon solely and if there is any suspicion of exhaust fumes reaching the cabin then the heating should be turned off and the cabin well ventilated. Another factor to consider is that the warm air system provides a path through the firewall for any fumes from a fire should one occur in the engine bay. This is why the heating system should be turned off before engine start, or if a fire in the engine bay is suspected.

Fresh air ventilation is provided through intakes in the leading edge of the wing feeding vents mounted adjacent to the front edge of the front seats. Obviously, this will only function when the aircraft is in motion; hence the reason for pilots leaving the door open on the ground on hot summer days whilst taxiing or waiting for departure. Overhead console vents can supplement the standard ventilation, which may also further benefit from an electrical blower. A switch adjacent to the warm air system control levers controls the blower. It is strongly recommended that if the warm air system is in use then the fresh air vents be operated as well to provide a balanced mix of fresh and warm air. This will help combat the nauseous and noxious effects of carbon monoxide should it find its way into the cabin and also help to prevent the pilot from becoming so warm and comfortable that he nods off! Or, maybe just a bit drowsy.

Heater Controls and Vents

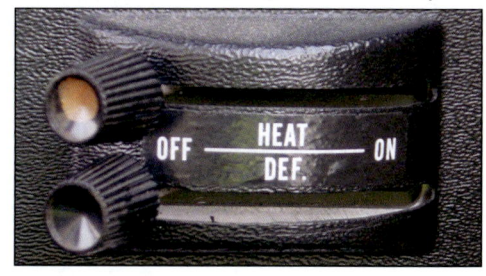

Seats and Safety Belts

The fabric trim of the later models is normally matched to the seat covering to make a quite pleasing comfortable interior with adjustable front seats and fixed twin seat in the rear. A bench type seat may be fitted in the rear of the normally two-seat cadet. The rearmost part of the cabin, behind the rear seats, forms the baggage area. To adjust the front seats fore and aft a bar beneath the front edge of the seat is lifted and if optional height adjustment is incorporated a lever on front corner of the seat is used to allow the seat to move up or down. The right seat also tips forward to allow access to the rear seats. All seats are fitted with a lap strap and the front seats additionally have a diagonal shoulder strap. The shoulder strap is of the inertia reel type, its operation can be checked by simply giving it a sharp tug, which should cause the reel to lock and prevent further movement if it is functioning correctly. The baggage area is also fitted with restraint straps for securing anything placed there. The weight allowed in the baggage area is a substantial 200lbs (90kgs), evenly distributed, for the Warrior and Archer variants. However, this allowance can only be used to the maximum, if, combined with the rest of the aircraft load the weight and balance of the aircraft remains within the allowable limits. This will be covered to a greater extent later. The Cadet has a maximum baggage load of only 50lbs (22kgs). For some flight manoeuvres the carriage of baggage is prohibited and this should be checked before flight.

Access Doors and remaining Cabin Features

As stated earlier the cabin is accessed by the single door on the right hand side via the black painted walkway. Externally a catch on the top and side of the door are used to open it, internally the two catches vary slightly in design depending upon the exact model. A handhold in the armrest enables the door to be pulled closed, which on early models would automatically latch the door; later models have a lever ahead of the armrest that is moved down into the locking position. The top catch is then moved to the locked position to secure the top of the door.

Typical Top Catch

Lever type door locking handle

If incorrectly latched the door may open in flight, sometimes following the aforementioned practice of leaving the door open on the ground during hot weather! This, however, should not prove to be too problematical to overcome as slowing the aircraft down to just below 90kts, with the DV window open and the cabin vents closed, should enable the door to be properly closed. However, this should not preoccupy the pilot at the expense of flying the aircraft. If unable to latch the door easily, maintain a safe slow speed and land as soon as practicable. Entry to and exiting the cabin is reasonably easy but due to the step down into the rather confined area of the cabin some people may need assistance; or guidance on what to hold on to and what might be damaged if they lever their whole bodyweight on it. Also ensure that only the black painted strengthened part of the wing is stood upon and use the handhold provided on the fuselage.

Normal Operating Procedures

Preamble

The Piper Warrior is a very easy, stable and forgiving aeroplane to fly, which makes it an ideal trainer and tourer alike. Very little in its normal operating procedures should give the student, or qualified pilot alike, cause for concern. Although the Warrior has few vices, like all aircraft, if operated incorrectly it is quite capable of, as a minimum, embarrassing the pilot. Although the cabin comfortably accommodates four adults with some baggage and the fuel tanks a capacity of up to 48 US gals, weight and balance needs to be checked to ensure the aircraft is operated within the correct loading limits. This is covered in a later section with the attention the subject deserves. Although some tips and advice on handling is given in this section nothing, however, should override the guidance given by a flying instructor familiar with the type, and this guide should act rather as reinforcement and a supplement to knowledge given during flying training.

Safe on the Ground

The common practice of parking light aircraft pointing into wind applies to the Warrior but it is less susceptible to damage from strong winds than high wing types like the Cessnas. However, in a strong wing it would still be possible for a Warrior to be flipped over on to its back if not parked and tied down correctly. If exposed to such winds then it should be tied down using the tie down points fitted under the wings. The tie down point under the tail should also be used if the wind direction is expected to change to blow from behind the aircraft, or if the aircraft is going to be unattended for some time. Another precaution, against wind damage, possible when the aircraft is parked on grass, is to dig out a small trough for the nose wheel to sit in which reduces the lifting power of the wings when wind blows over them. As the Warrior is not provided with a control lock it is important to park into wind to prevent to control surfaces from being blown about and causing possible damage. Also the pressure head should be covered when the aircraft is parked to prevent the ingress of bugs and other airborne contamination that could affect the function of the pitot-static instruments due to a blockage of the tubes. The parking brake should also be applied. A cover if available should also be fitted, in summer this helps to prevent the cabin becoming an oven before you get in the aircraft. In winter it will save having to de-frost the windows on those rather fresh mornings when Jack Frost has paid a visit! And that large single door that wraps around into the roof structure also has a habit of leaking on to the right hand seat during heavy rain, just where the instructor sits! Not much you can do about it in the air but on the ground the cover will make a big difference.

Starting

Starting the Warrior is fairly straightforward. Select the fuel tank with the least contents, unless empty! Ensure carb heat is off and mixture is rich. With the master switch on, open the throttle about ¼" - ½" (5-10mm) prime the engine using 3 - 4 strokes (engine cold) and then turn the magneto key switch until the starter engages and turns the engine. (Note, with a warm engine priming should not be required). After starting the engine rpm should be adjusted to about 1200rpm. If the engine does not start after, say, 10 - 15 seconds of cranking then it is probable that the engine is either under or over primed. It is better to stop cranking the engine and decide on a further course of action than continue. If during the attempt to start the engine it fired erratically and puffs of black smoke were seen to come from the exhaust, then a flooded or over primed engine is the likely cause. If this is the case, then fully open the throttle and select ICO on the mixture control then operate the starter again. As the engine starts retard the throttle and move the mixture to the fully rich position. This is best done with three hands! Alternatively leave starting for 10 - 15 minutes to allow the fuel to evaporate. If, however, during start the engine does not fire at all then it is probably under primed for the conditions (i.e. cold) and further priming will be required. Do not try "pumping" the throttle as this can cause an excess of fuel to collect in the carburettor with the attendant fire risk. Also, the engine does not "suck in" the fuel provided by the primer so well with the throttle wide open.

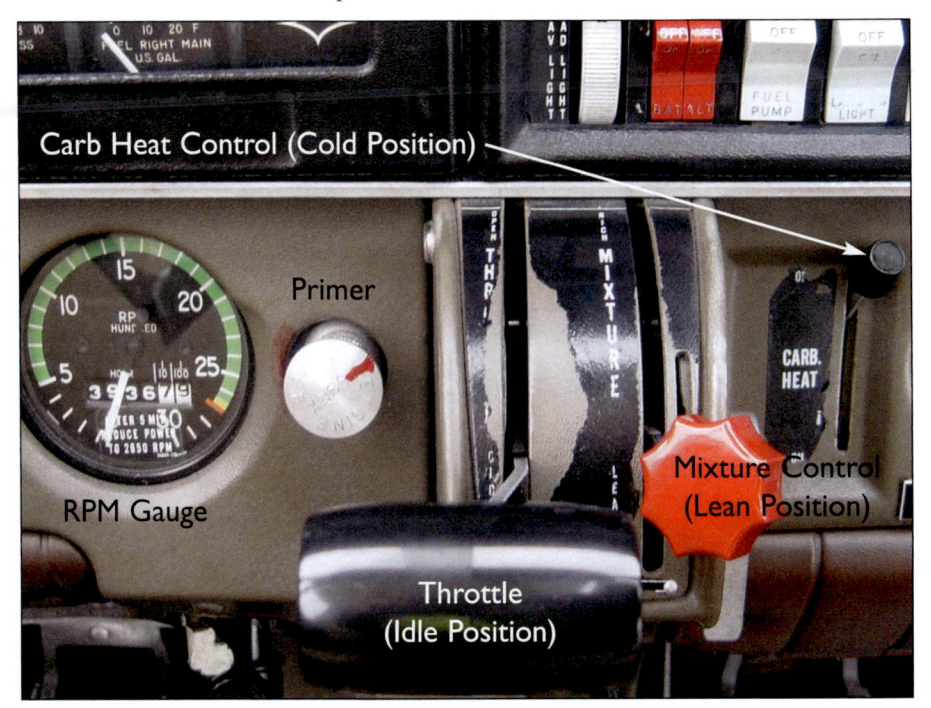

The aircraft is fitted with a warning light that illuminates when the starter motor is operated. If it remains on after starting the engine, damage to the starter motor and electrical system could occur and so the engine should be immediately shut down. Assuming this is not the case, then the oil pressure gauge should be checked next, to ensure that the oil pressure is rising within 30 seconds to within the green arc. Again if this is not apparent then shut down the engine before serious damage is caused. Other system gauges should also be checked at this point such as suction and ammeter gauges, followed by other checks set out in the "After start check list"

Taxying

The Warrior is very manoeuvrable on the ground due to the direct linkage between the rudder pedals and the nose wheel. Although at first this may feel a bit heavy. The direct linkage also prevents full and free movement of the rudder from being checked until the aircraft is moving. The turning circle can be improved, if necessary, by the use of differential braking and a little extra power, assuming toe brakes are fitted; although caution is needed to prevent total lock-up of a wheel, which can cause tyre scrubbing. If toe brakes are not fitted then using full rudder deflection and the handbrake with extra power will reduce the turning circle a bit but not as much as differential braking. All the brakes should be checked before taxying very far or getting too fast. It is also normal practice to test the brake function shortly after commencing taxying, although a brake pressure test could be carried out before moving off.

Taxying in a crosswind should not present any problems due to the nose wheel being directly linked to the rudder pedals, although some rudder pressure may be required to prevent a weathercock action.

When reducing speed the throttle should be closed first, but following this it should be reset to 1200 rpm to help prevent spark plug fouling. The speed used for taxying depends on the surface being traversed. When crossing a grass surface particular care needs to be taken to avoid potential damage being caused by travelling too fast over a surface that may be rutted, uneven or have soft patches.

The diagram below shows the recommended positions for the control column depending on the prevailing wind conditions.

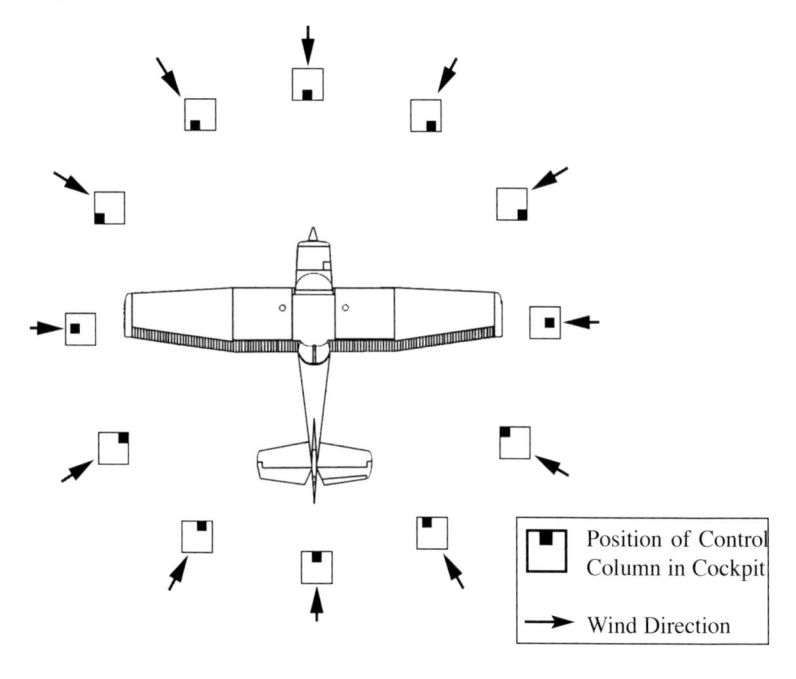

Take-Off

Before take-off, a normal set of power and pre take-off checks is carried out. Normally the aircraft is positioned into wind to carry out these checks, which aids engine cooling. Also, the controls will be buffeted about if the wind is blowing from behind the aircraft whilst the checks are completed. With the aircraft in the correct place, the fuel tank with most fuel is selected and then normally the engine is opened up to 2000rpm and the carb heat checked first, with a drop of approx 50rpm being a typical and correct result. It should be remembered, that as explained in the engine section the carb heat supplies the engine with an unfiltered source of air and should therefore be used only as and when necessary. Otherwise dust and other airborne particles will pass into the engine, which would lead to increased wear. Following the carb heat the magnetos are checked individually. The maximum permissible drop is 125rpm with difference between the two of no more than 50rpm. Although a lower rpm is witnessed when operating on one magneto the engine should still run smoothly and if not then a fouled spark plug may be the problem. It is sometimes possible to clear a fouled plug by maintaining the rpm at 2000 (with magnetos on both) and leaning off the mixture to give maximum rpm for a short time. Then return the mixture to the rich position and recheck the magnetos. If the problem has disappeared it is fine to carry on, if not then the aircraft requires the attention of an engineer as problem may be more serious. Following a successful magneto check oil pressure and temperature, suction and ammeter indications are checked at 2000 rpm too. The throttle is then closed to check the idling rpm is between 500-700 and that oil pressure and ammeter readings are within limits. Following this the pre take-off checks are carried out from the check list to ensure the aircraft is correctly set up for take-off, then review the wind direction for crosswind component and its potential affect. The maximum demonstrated crosswind is 17 kts although each pilot should recognise his own limits and currency. It is important to be able to calculate quickly and mentally the approximate crosswind from a given wind velocity. One method (and there are several) is to use the face of a watch to aid the calculation. The diagram below may help to see how this is done. First of all, work out the angular difference between the runway direction and the wind direction. Then, looking at our watch face imagine the 15 minute position to represent 15 deg., 30 minutes / 30 deg, 45 minutes / 45 deg, 60 minutes / 60 deg. These increments also represent ¼, ½, ¾ and a full watch face respectively. We then return to the wind velocity given, use the angular difference between the wind and runway to arrive at the fraction of a watch face and multiply the wind speed by this fraction. E.g. wind 30 deg off the runway at 18 kts. 30 deg = 30 min = ½ a watch face, therefore ½ x 18 = 9 kts of crosswind. A quick and simple method to work out the crosswind component. Anything more than 60 deg would be treated as all crosswind. Although not mathematically pure, it is good enough and easy to apply even when on final approach to land or just prior to take-off.

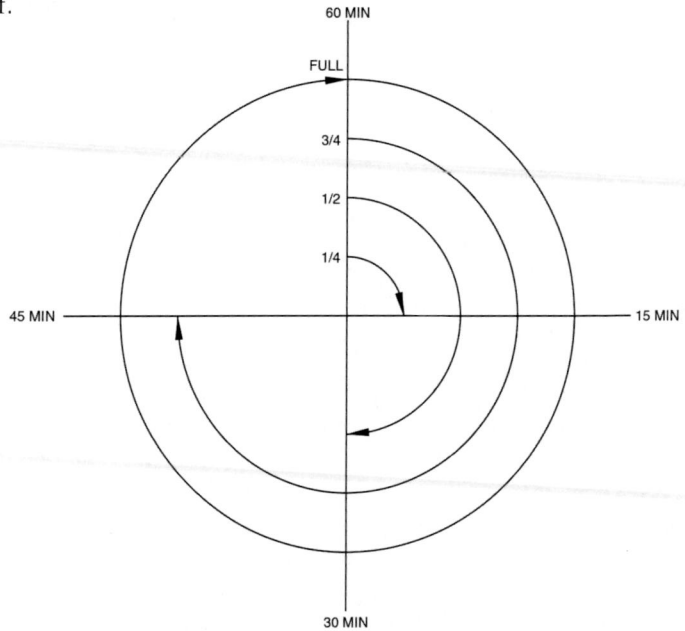

WIND 30 DEG FROM R/W DIRECTION IS READ AS 30 MINUTES ON
OUR WATCH FACE AND THEREFORE HALF THE WIND SPEED

Following the line up on the runway ensure heels are on the floor to prevent inadvertent brake application and smoothly increase the power to full. As a guide the throttle should be opened from normal idle (1200 rpm) to full power over a count of about 4. This avoids too rapid an increase in power, which is not good for the engine or directional control of the aircraft. Once the aircraft is directionally stable then a check to see that full power is being developed, about 2350 rpm at this stage and that oil pressure and temperature are normal. Also check that the airspeed is increasing.

For a normal take-off the nose wheel is lifted off the runway at about 50 kts and climb away at 65 kts/75 kts. If a short field performance takeoff is required, then 25 deg of flap (2 stages) is used and an initial climb speed of 60 kts to give best angle of climb. After the initial climb of say 200/300 ft the airspeed should be increased and the flaps retracted. The best rate of climb (Vy) is achieved at 79 kts and the best angle (Vx) at 64 kts. As the engine is at full power during the climb and the airspeed is relatively low, the engine oil temperature and pressure should be monitored in accordance with normal practice. Changing to a cruise climb at 85-90 kts improves the airflow around the engine and the view ahead without seriously affecting the rate of climb and could be adopted once a safe altitude had been passed.

Cruising

With reference to the performance graph below it can be seen that there can be significant differences in fuel consumption depending upon what power setting is used and altitude flown.

PA-28-161

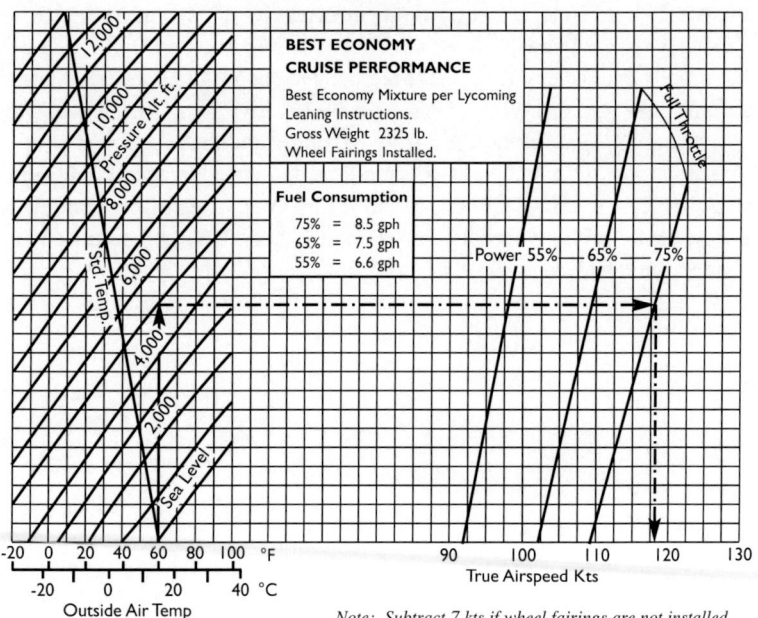

BEST ECONOMY CRUISE PERFORMANCE

Best Economy Mixture per Lycoming Leaning Instructions.
Gross Weight 2325 lb.
Wheel Fairings Installed.

Fuel Consumption
75% = 8.5 gph
65% = 7.5 gph
55% = 6.6 gph

Note: Subtract 7 kts if wheel fairings are not installed

Example:

    Cruise Pressure Altitude: 5000 ft
    Cruise OAT: 60°F
    Cruise Power: 75% Best Power Mixture
    Cruise Speed: 118 kts TAS

Typically 55% to 65% power would be used, this gives reasonable fuel consumption and 95 to 105kts of airspeed. The choice is yours! But an important planning issue is the endurance expected and the endurance achieved, which not only lies with the power and altitude selected but correct use of the mixture control, as we observed earlier in the section referring to the leaning procedure. More of this topic is discussed in the performance section on cruise performance. During any flight it is of the utmost importance to maintain good engine management throughout, as accidents, as a result of poor fuel management or carburettor ice detection still feature highly in AAIB reports. As mentioned earlier the fuel gauges are not highly accurate and any pre-flight check should include a visual check and careful calculation of the amount of fuel on board. Then ensure that it is enough for the flight, taxying, take-off, landing, diversion if necessary and some in reserve. Also, one should bear in mind that try as we might to achieve the book performance figures, we probably won't, as our aircraft is unlikely to be in the same mint condition as the one used to produce the figures and we are also unlikely to have the skill of the test pilot! One thing that doesn't require the skill of a test pilot, just diligent airmanship, is that of fuel management. You have to make sure that the fuel you do have in the tanks can reach the engine. Simple as it may sound, a periodic check of the fuel level in each tank should be made and the fuller tank selected to maintain the lateral balance. When changing tanks the electric fuel pump should be turned on first, then select the required tank, leave the pump on and check the fuel pressure after 15-20 seconds, finally, if all is well, switch off the fuel pump. If not, go back to the original tank before switching off the fuel pump. If at any time fuel pressure is lost, then the electric pump should immediately be used to restore fuel supply to the engine, provided that there is fuel in the selected tank! It cannot pump what is not there! If this were to happen to you, you can be safe in the knowledge that you are not the first! But making a forced landing with no fuel in one tank and plenty in the other, is not the most imaginative way to make it into an AAIB report.

Of course, fuel and carburettor ice are not the only engine factors to consider. The general health of the engine is displayed on the oil temperature and pressure gauges, and audibly, by the way it sounds. An immense silence from up front tells you an awful lot about the health of the engine! However, by careful monitoring we may spot an impending problem before it gets to that stage. When oil is cold it is quite a viscous fluid like condensed milk! But as it gets hot it thins out to be more like normal milk! And the hotter it gets the thinner or more watery it gets. Inside an engine one of the most important tasks oil has to perform is that of lubrication. To do this, as we saw before, it is pumped around the engine by the oil pump to those parts requiring it. Having lubricated the relevant parts it leaks out back to the sump. The problem we have is that the thinner the oil, the easier it is for it to leak back to the sump before performing the lubrication; and also to leak internally around the pump, preventing it from producing the correct pressure in the first place. So, if we observe a high oil temperature reading combined with a low oil pressure our engine is likely to very shortly to be in the initial throes of self-destruction followed by that immense silence!

Therefore, some immediate action is called for. It may be that it is a particularly hot day and you have just got to the top of a long slow climb without observing the gauges in the climb. Lowering the nose attitude and reducing power to the cruise may restore things to normal. However, serious consideration should be given to the idea of terminating the flight as soon as possible. If, however, if there is an erroneous reading on one gauge only then it may just be a faulty gauge or sensor, but in any case the pilot's best course of action would probably be to divert to the nearest airfield for further inspection. During the cruise, monitoring of other system gauges like the suction and ammeter should also of course be carried out to warn the pilot of problems in those areas. The stability designed into the Warrior, combined with effective controls and efficient trimmers make it a delightful tourer. The addition, however, of a rudder trimmer sometimes gets overlooked by a pilot more familiar with those types that do not have this facility. The rudder trim can be an advantage if used correctly, but left in the position that the last pilot used it, may be a distinct pain in the xxxx - well, leg really! Corrective rudder is likely to be required to maintain balance in the cruise. Various options like electric elevator trim and autopilot can also be found on the Warrior, and the pilot should ensure that he is fully conversant with their respective operational uses, limitations and how to disengage them.

Stalling

A stall in the Warrior is conventional and quite docile. There is very little buffet in the clean, power off, stall and if held in the stall during training this can be demonstrated, together with the typical nodding action of the nose of the aircraft. Recovery, using a standard stall recovery technique with power would typically require about 100 -150ft once initiated. The stalling speed in this condition varies a bit between models and with the position of the centre of gravity and weight but would be around 50 -55kts.

The flight manual lists the stall speeds with a forward and rearward C of G and various flap settings, all of which will vary the actual stall speed.

An electric stall warner is fitted with an activating vane on the port wing. The warning horn typically sounds at 5-10kts above the stall.

Stalling with power and flap or in a turn is likely to induce a wing drop at the stall unless the aircraft is kept in balance, which would reduce this tendency. However, dealt with correctly under the guidance of an instructor this should not prove too difficult to master.

Prior to any stalling exercise the weight and centre of gravity position should be checked to certify that limits of the operational category (either normal or utility) are not exceeded.

Spinning

It is prohibited intentionally to spin the Warrior, Cadet or Archer. Some mild aerobatic manoeuvres are allowed with the aircraft in the Utility category. However, should an unintentional spin develop then the pilot should be familiar with the recovery.

Essentially, the recovery would involve ensuring the throttle is closed, flaps are up, identify the direction of spin and apply full rudder in the opposite direction to the spin. Check the ailerons are neutral and move the control column centrally fully forward. When the spin stops centralise the rudder and ease out of the ensuing dive!

As intentional spinning is prohibited in the Warrior and therefore not practised in the type, it would be a good idea to obtain some experience of the manoeuvre in an appropriate type as there is no substitute for proper training. If nothing else it would intensify one's attention to the aircraft's behaviour when carrying out manoeuvres that bring the aircraft within spitting distance of a stall! Remember, "Do-It-Yourself" aerobatic training is about as clever as do-it-yourself brain surgery!

Approach and Landing

During a descent is another time to remind ourselves that power plus attitude equals performance. The aircraft can descend with power varied from idle (glide descent) to around 2000rpm (cruise descent). Which you choose to use depends upon the circumstances. For a given airspeed, the greater the reduction in power, the greater the rate of descent. When using power settings of less than 2000 rpm it is usual to select full carb heat first to prevent carb icing occurring, reselecting cold air if full power is required for a "Go Around". Lowering flaps will also increase the rate of descent.

Following normal pre-landing checks the flaps are deployed during the initial stages of approach, lowering flap causes the nose initially to pitch up, which should be prevented, followed by a reduction in airspeed. Usually 25° of flap would be selected on base leg of a circuit and 40° on final approach. This is a very important time to ensure that the aircraft is correctly trimmed as there is significant trim change when flaps are deployed and it is highly likely that the aircraft will be flying at a low airspeed. Throughout the descent a scan should be maintained to ensure that the aircraft is doing what we intended in terms of performance and correcting for any errors. This can be usefully practised at altitude away from the pressure of a landing.

The Warrior is fairly easy to land but it can quickly go very wrong if the approach is not flown correctly. Of course the second part of that statement applies to any aircraft, although the Warrior is quite forgiving. As with any aircraft, the trick is for the pilot to be ahead of the aircraft. Like any sport, anticipation is the name of the game. The question on our mind should always be, what is it going to do next? A similar thought process used when playing a game of, say, tennis or squash. If this is considered then the pilot can make a control input exactly when it is required, as there will always be a delay between control input and response of the aircraft. That said, in normal conditions if the approach is flown at the correct speed of around 70kts reducing to 65kts over the numbers, flaring at the appropriate height (which can only learnt by demonstration), closing the throttle and holding off until a touch down on the main wheels first is assured; then an acceptable landing is likely to be the result. As discussed before, the main wheels are designed to take more of the landing load than the nose wheel and care should therefore be taken to protect the nose wheel during the initial landing phase. Most problems arise from approaching at an inappropriate speed, the aircraft being aimed at the threshold or numbers with little regard for the aircraft speed or wind conditions. This is likely to result in "ballooning" at the flare or "bouncing" on touch down, both of which should elicit an immediate "Go Around". Of course there are many problems that can plague a pilot when landing, which can lead to a certain amount of frustration. However, if you do have problems analysis by a flying instructor and guidance in the correct techniques should ensure this is overcome effectively. Landing accidents due to mishandling in this critical phase of flight are quite common, as mentioned earlier, although quite avoidable. Firstly, by using the correct technique to land and secondly, to have the presence of mind, airmanship, to "Go Around" if it starts to go wrong. Remember, anticipation, if you wait until it has gone wrong it's probably too late and you will need some assistance to retrieve the propeller and nose leg from the runway!

Should a Go Around be necessary, then the throttle should be opened to full power over a period of a couple of seconds. This action prevents the accelerator pump jet fitted to the carburettor from delivering an over rich mixture that could cause a loss of power if the throttle were opened rapidly. Only moderate forward pressure on the control is required to prevent the nose attitude rising too far when full power is applied for the Go Around. Raising the 40° stage of flap to 25° at the first opportunity is also a must, to improve the climb performance. The remaining flap should be raised in stages at a safe height when the aircraft is maintaining a positive rate of climb. If for some reason the flaps become inoperable, then a flapless approach and landing will be required, with the approach flown at a slightly higher airspeed of 70-75kts. In this case the hold off would be much longer with a much less pronounced flare and therefore requiring a much longer landing distance. After touchdown on the main wheels, the back pressure on the control column, required for the correct landing attitude, is gradually relaxed allowing the nose wheel to come into contact gently with the runway. With the good directional control that the Warrior possesses it is relatively easy to keep straight during the roll out.

Performance

Preamble and terminology used in this section.

An aircraft's performance will vary greatly depending upon a number of factors. A performance table or graph will normally give the pilot the basic raw data for, say, a take-off distance. This figure however may not take into consideration the difference in aircraft performance that may be achieved in conditions that differ vastly from those of the test aircraft. The Warrior graphs enable allowances for temperature, pressure altitude, weight and wind. Any other variations from the stated conditions should be assessed and their effect on the aircraft's subsequent performance calculated. This process is called factoring. The CAA in AIC 67/2002 (Pink 36) gives guidance information on light aircraft performance. I strongly recommend this as further reading on the subject, if you are not already familiar with the document. It sets forth general information on the subject and also correction factors that are recommended for use when adjusting raw data performance figures for actual conditions. How the pilot loads and handles the aircraft and manages the engine will also affect the performance achieved. In the next section we will deal with how to load the Warrior correctly and the loading limits. The flight manual section on performance assumes that the aircraft load is correctly distributed to maintain the centre of gravity within the prescribed limits. The tables and graphs in the performance section are used by the pilot to obtain the information necessary to achieve a particular performance, be it climb, cruise or descent etc. However, it would be wise to remember that the information provided within this section would have been achieved by a very experienced test pilot in a brand new aircraft! If you and your aircraft are not in the same category then additional allowances need to be made for safety, especially in the take-off and landing phases. For this reason it would be prudent to 'factor', or multiply any take-off or landing performance figure, obtained from the tables, by the recommended public transport safety factors. These being 1.33 and 1.43 respectively. There may be other reasons for further factoring such as surface condition, as we shall see later. Although sample tables are reproduced in this booklet, to demonstrate their use, always ensure that you use the data from the actual flight manual of the aircraft being used for operational purposes. There may well be a CAA amendment sheet for certain performance criteria inserted into the flight manual/POH. Additionally, there may be graphs in the POH that already include the CAA safety factor. Furthermore, you may be operating an aircraft under JAR OPS requirements, which needs different factoring values. In the near future the slightly different JAR OPS values will supersede the CAA safety factors, therefore check which figures your particular operator recommends. Each table or graph in the P.O.H. will be accompanied by a list of conditions that applied to the aircraft when that data was produced. So, any variation from these conditions needs to be considered and if necessary adjusted for, or 'factored'. It is important that you read any notes that precede the performance graphs and don't dive in making incorrect assumptions.

At the end of the day we must ensure that any distances (be it take off or landing) that our aircraft requires is less than that which is available, otherwise we are asking for trouble. Many smaller airfields (unlicensed) do not publish declared distances (apart from the actual length of the runway itself) or information on obstacles that may be just off the end of the runway. It would therefore be prudent in those circumstances to use the runway length as the take-off distance available (TODA) and not simply the take-off run available (TORA). In commercial flying further calculations are made for multi-engined aircraft to know at what point a take-off can be aborted and still bring the aircraft to a halt on the runway or stopway. Beyond that point the aircraft must continue with the take-off, even with engine failure. With one engine our options are rather more limited! But we should still have some idea of a point on the runway at which we should be airborne or if not, be able to bring the aircraft to a halt without creating another aircraft shaped entrance to the airfield at the end of the runway! This sort of problem may be worse on a wet grass runway with difficult braking conditions. To this end consider the accelerate - stop distance of your aircraft and the emergency distance available. The distance it takes to stop the aircraft can be, (to a great degree) worked out from the landing run required graph or table of an aircraft POH. The above may at first appear to require an awful lot of work but it will provide you with the knowledge to make informed, rather than guesswork decisions.

(Illustrations of TORA, TODA and LDA LRA)

TORR   Takeoff run required. Runway length required to become airborne.

TODR   Take-off distance required. Distance required to become airborne and clear an imaginary barrier 50ft high.

LRR   Landing run required. Runway length required from touch down to achieving a full stop.

LDR   Landing distance required. Distance required to touch down after clearing an imaginary 50ft barrier plus the landing run required.

TORA   Take off run available.

TODA   Take off distance available.

LRA   Landing run available.

LDA   Landing distance available.

Pressure Altitude

For airfield elevation purposes this equates to the altitude displayed on the altimeter with the aircraft on the ground and the sub-scale set to the standard setting of 1013mb.

With reference to the extract from AIC 67/2002 shown below we can see the sort of factors that will affect an aircraft's performance and how we can adjust for them. However, this is probably best illustrated by working through an example as shown below.

AIC 67/2002

Para 1.3 Aeroplane Performance is subject to many variables including:
    Aeroplane weight
    Aerodrome altitude
    Temperature
    Wind
    Runway length, slope and surface
    Flap setting
    Humidity

Para 5.8 Humidity
    High humidity has an adverse affect on performance and this is usually taken into account during certification, however, there may be a correction factor applicable to your aeroplane. Consult the manual. Apart from the humidity issue, the above variables can be factored for and flap setting is given as a condition of the performance table.

Take-off Performance

It can be seen from the performance graphs below, that the graph allows the pilot to obtain a take-off distance or ground roll factored directly for temperature, pressure altitude, weight and wind speed. This figure is then adjusted as required for any remaining factors that could affect the take-off distance. One of the easiest ways to understand any of the performance graphs is to work through an example. So, let us assume we are going to visit an unfamiliar airfield, Picture Book Airfield, for the first time! We have been diligent enough to obtain the airfield information and conditions needed to carry out our calculations. Then, as take-off distances are generally greater than landing we are firstly going to check that we will be able to get airborne following a successful arrival.

Picture Book airfield information and current conditions:

Runway	-	900 m
Surface	-	Short dry grass
Elevation	-	390 ft
Temp.	-	+15°C
Wind	-	Calm
QNH	-	993mb.
A/c weight	-	2200 lbs.

Four graphs for take-off are generally provided covering TODR, TORR both with and without flap. Ensure the correct graph is being studied for the outcome required. The graph reproduced below gives the TODR with 25° flaps (second notch), as this will give the shortest TODR and generally recommended for departures from grass airfields.

Whichever graph is used a line will have to be drawn or other marks made to follow a path across the grid, which are best done in pencil so that it can be erased afterwards. An improvement on this method however, is to use a strip of transparency film with straight line photocopied on to it and rotate it around drawing pin placed in the graph at the appropriate point as you work across the graph.

Sample only - not for operational use.

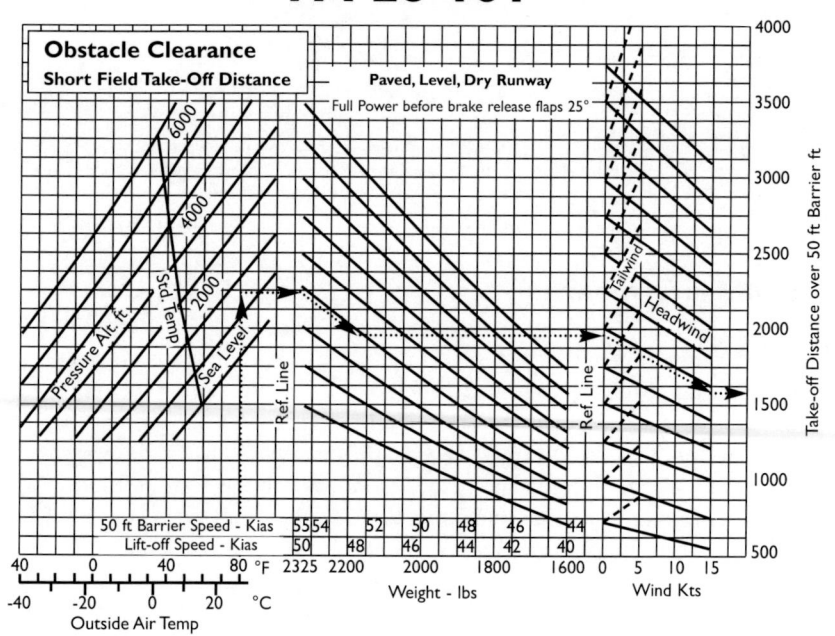

PA-28-161

Obstacle Clearance
Short Field Take-Off Distance — Paved, Level, Dry Runway
Full Power before brake release flaps 25°

Note: the conditions given on the graph. Paved, level, dry runway, flaps 25° and full power before releasing brakes for take-off.

Looking at the Take-off Performance graph above, we enter on the bottom left with the air temperature and go directly up to the pressure altitude. Therefore the pressure altitude needs to be calculated before we can go any further.

So, we can either set 1013mb on the altimeter sub-scale and read off the pressure altitude, a bit tricky if you are not already there! Or calculate it using the approximate figure of 30ft per millibar.

As the airfield pressure is lower than standard, 1013mb, then the resulting performance will be as if the airfield were 1013 - 993 (20mb) higher than it actually is. We can then convert this 20mb to a height (30 x 20) of 600ft. Add to this its actual elevation of 390ft and finally arrive at our pressure altitude of 990ft!

Back to the graph. Entering with the air temperature of 15°C, move vertically up to the pressure altitude of 990ft (1000ft is close enough). Then go horizontally across to the reference line for the aircraft weight and parallel diagonally down the weight lines with your pencil line until it intersects the vertical line for the weight of the loaded aircraft 2200lbs. From here we move horizontally across the graph to the head or tail wind reference line, where again we parallel the appropriate line until the vertical line that represents the value of the wind speed is met. Note that headwind lines are drawn going down diagonally to the right and tailwind lines diagonally upwards and these are already factored by the appropriate amount so that actual wind speed can be used. When the vertical line representing the wind speed is met we move horizontally to the right to read off the Take-off Distance. In our case with nil wind we can go directly from the wind reference to the Take-off Distance. The same procedure is used for the other performance graphs to obtain the outcome on the right hand side of the graph.

Our example produces a TODR of 1600ft.
To convert this figure to metres 1600 x .03048 = 488m.

As the Warrior graph effectively factors for the temperature, pressure altitude, weight and wind directly we now only need to factor for the grass (as the conditions state a paved runway) and then finally the recommended safety factor.

From the table below, reproduced from AIC 67/2002, we can derive the factors or multipliers that we need to apply to our basic TODR to obtain the correct value for our particular set of conditions at Picture Book Airfield. Therefore, in our case, all we need to do is multiply the basic TODR by the factor for grass (1.2) and safety (1.33).

Take-off Performance Factors

Condition	Increase in take off distance	Multiplication Factor
A 10% increase in aircraft weight	20%	1.20
An increase of 1000ft in aerodrome altitude	10%	1.10
An increase of 10°C in ambient temperature	10%	1.10
Dry grass * Up to 20cm (8") (on firm soil)	20%	1.20
Wet grass * Up to 20cm (8") (on firm soil)	30%	1.35
A 2% uphill slope*	10%	1.10
A tailwind component of 10% of lift off speed	20%	1.20
Soft ground or snow*	25% or more	1.25+

Effect on ground roll will be proportionately greater.

Basic TODR 488m.
Further factors: Short dry grass   1.2
                  Take-off safety   1.33
Therefore, Factored TODR: 488 × 1.2 × 1.33 = 779m

If a take-off without using flap is considered then the TODR works out to be 875m (including the factors for grass and safety). So it can be seen that the take-off distance reduces by 96m if flaps are used.

However, this assumes that the correct lift off speed is used for the particular weight of the aircraft; this is also displayed on the graph. In our case would be 48kts and 53kts over the imaginary barrier gradually accelerating to the best rate of climb speed and retracting the flaps as required. Nevertheless, there should be no problem on this particular day getting our particular aircraft off this particular airfield. It remains now, to work out the amount of runway that will be required to land our aircraft safely.

Another pause for thought though would be to consider how much runway you need to stop your beloved steed if you decide to abandon the take off at nearly lift off speed? Some idea can be gleaned from the landing run table as you will be at a similar speed. Even more runway please!

Landing Performance

As we have seen, the take-off distance an aircraft requires can vary considerably when it is operated in differing conditions. So too is the landing distance. Once again when planning a trip, in particular, to an unfamiliar airfield it would be very poor airmanship not to carry out a landing performance calculation. AIC 67/2002 also gives us guidance in how to adjust the landing distance required for the variables that will affect it. For convenience the table from that AIC is reproduced below.

Landing Performance Factors

Condition	Increase in landing distance	Multiplication Factor
A 10% increase in aircraft weight	10%	1.10
An increase of 1000ft in aerodrome altitude	5%	1.05
An increase of 10°C in ambient temperature	5%	1.05
A wet paved runway	15%	1.15
Dry grass * Up to 20cm (8") (on firm soil)	15%	1.15
Wet grass * Up to 20cm (8") (on firm soil)	35%	1.35
A 2% downhill slope*	10%	1.10
A tailwind component of 10% of landing speed	20%	1.20
Soft ground or snow*	25% or more	1.25+

Effect on ground roll will be proportionately greater.

So, working through our example at Picture Book Airfield again, we will calculate our actual LDR and LRR.

Assume airfield and aircraft conditions are as above and approach using short field technique. The flight manual considers this to be:

Power	Idle
Flaps	40°
Approach speed	63kts
Touch down speed	Stall

After touch down flaps retracted and maximum braking applied.

Therefore, following a similar procedure used in the take-off performance graph, enter the graph on the bottom left with the air temperature (15°). Go vertically up to the pressure altitude (1000ft), then horizontally across to the wind lines (interpolate if necessary), dropping down vertically to read off the landing distance. On this graph two groups of wind lines are provided to enable either landing distance or landing run to be read off.

Sample only - not for operational use.

PA-28-161

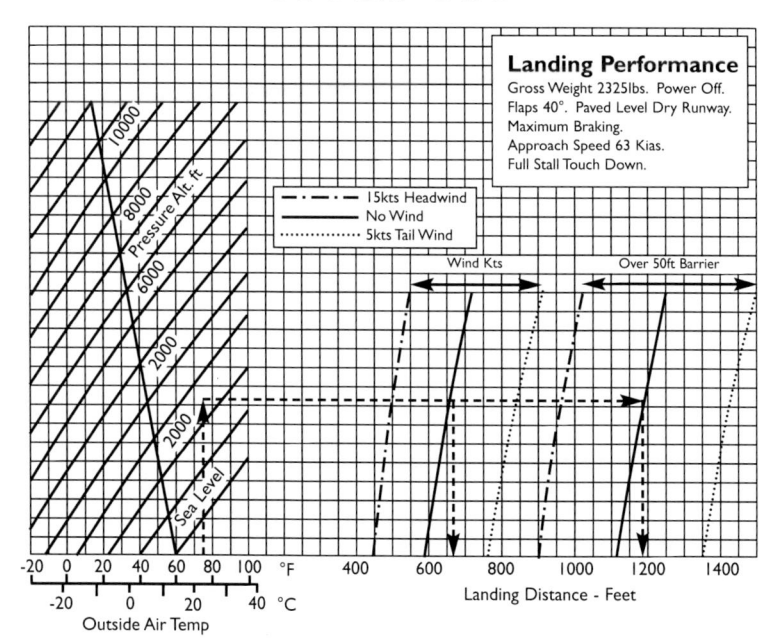

Landing Performance
Gross Weight 2325lbs. Power Off.
Flaps 40°. Paved Level Dry Runway.
Maximum Braking.
Approach Speed 63 Kias.
Full Stall Touch Down.

Our example gives us a LDR of 1130ft or ground roll of 610ft.

It can be seen printed on the graph that it assumes the aircraft is at maximum weight. But unlike the take-off performance graph there are no factoring allowance lines for a decreased landing weight.

As in the case for take off, further factoring for the grass surface (1.15) and a recommended safety margin (1.43) is required with the information from the table above.

Converting the LDR of 1130ft to metres gives us a basic LDR of 345m.
Further factors: Short dry grass   1.15
                             Landing safety   1.43
Therefore, factored   LDR: 345 × 1.15 × 1.43 = 567m.
The LRR works out to be 610ft or 186m
Factoring for grass and safety gives 319m.

Since the LDA is 900m and our LDR is 567m there should not be a problem, as long as we fly the aircraft in the correct manner so as to achieve the performance figures quoted. Therefore you might need to review the correct short field technique recommended in the flight manual. Approaching at 10kts above the correct speed, with only partial flap and touching down well down the runway is a guaranteed recipe for unintentional hedge cutting in the shape of an aeroplane! I think they call it topiary, but best not done with a propeller! If the approach does not seem to be working out when you get there, may-be it's not your day, but don't let any pressure force you to try and land. Go home and practise your short field technique on a long runway first, make up a spot landing competition for yourself; and only accept perfection! The runway I have used as an illustration is not particularly short and there are many that offer far more limiting distances, but with the right conditions and experience these offer interesting places to visit. Carrying out the performance calculations is only one half of the story; the other is your ability to fly the aeroplane in the correct manner so as to achieve the performance. Only you can answer that and do not be too proud to ask an instructor for a lesson on how to achieve the outcome you desire. Instructors are not there just for basic training, but also to help you develop your piloting skills as you acquire more experience, remember, we are all learning always. This reminds me to mention that with all the foregoing completed and assessed we have not even mentioned the effect of a crosswind on the proceedings or that of a gusty day. This should also be considered. Is it a narrow runway or a slightly scaled down Heathrow? In my capacity as a Flight Instructor Course instructor I am frequently presented with pilots holding a commercial licence who can't land for toffee in a crosswind. We definitely just arrive! And, as we have to operate off a fairly narrow runway it is a rather important skill that may not be required so much at a larger aerodrome. But operating into or out of a smaller runway it takes on a more important significance. This is another skill that can easily be improved and result in an immense feeling of satisfaction, conquering a sometimes, mystifying and elusive goal.

Cruise Performance

Cruise performance is affected by many things not least by the power setting and the use of mixture control. As seen earlier (in the carburettor section) in the sample engine performance graph, fuel consumption will vary enormously depending on the power setting used. Again it would be sensible to make a correction factor for fuel flow, due to flying an old aircraft and possible pilot inaccuracies in adjusting the mixture in accordance with the flight manual. As well as the cruise performance graphs illustrating the expected airspeed and specific fuel consumption against altitude, temperature and power setting; the flight manual provides profile graphs for endurance and range. As with most things in life you don't get something for nothing. The faster you fly, the less distance you can cover and the shorter is the time that you can spend in the air on a given amount of fuel. The cruise performance graphs show how far and for how long you could expect to fly at a given power setting at a particular altitude. I say, "could expect" because of the factors that may affect the endurance or range. Factors, which the pilot should bear in mind and make sensible allowances for. One important piece of information that can seen in the engine performance graph is that varying the power from 55% to 75% can increase the fuel consumption by as much as 30%! So with just this piece of knowledge, if you have to hold somewhere for whatever reason, do so at a sensible power setting that conserves fuel. You might need the time. In any event always plan to have enough fuel for your trip (factored for you and your aeroplane) to hold for at least 45 minutes and to get you to an alternative destination and still some in the tanks after landing.

The Warrior manual provides a graph showing engine power developed for a particular RPM, altitude and temperature and various cruise performance graphs. If the graphs are studied a power setting can be chosen depending upon the requirements for airspeed and fuel consumption, the prevailing temperature and altitude flown. The difference between best power and best economy mixture should also be appreciated as it has a significant effect on the fuel consumed. If, in expectation of your leaning technique achieving best economy, you actually adjust for best power, the fuel consumption will be around 18% higher than expected. In my experience most pilots, in ignorance, lean the mixture to the best power mixture, if they lean the mixture at all! If the mixture remains unleaned then the fuel consumption will be significantly higher still.

Therefore, when fuel planning take this information into account rather than using a blasé ball park figure, which is fine so long as you are aware under what conditions the ball park figure applies. An example of a Best Power graph and Best Economy graph are illustrated on page 75. A few moments of study would reveal that the best power mixture will give a few more knots of airspeed at the expense of a significant increase in the fuel burn.

Sample only - not for operational use.

PA-28-161

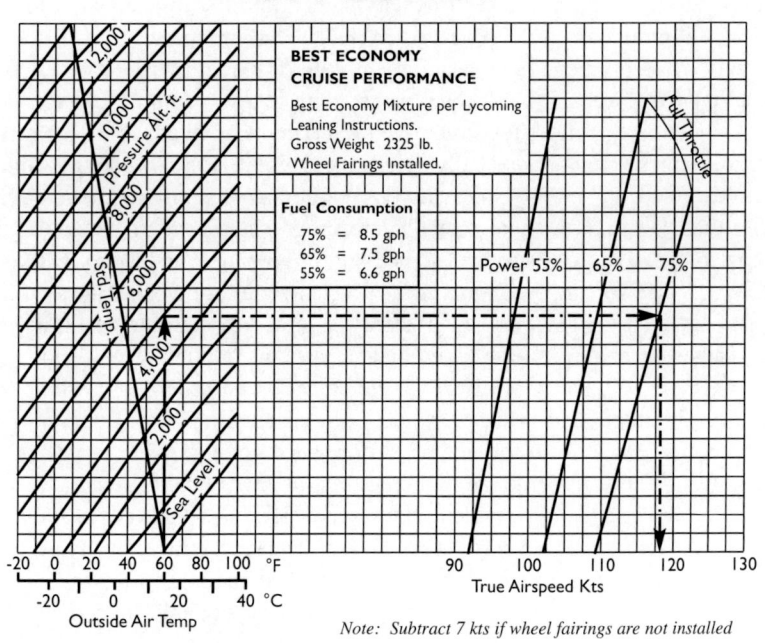

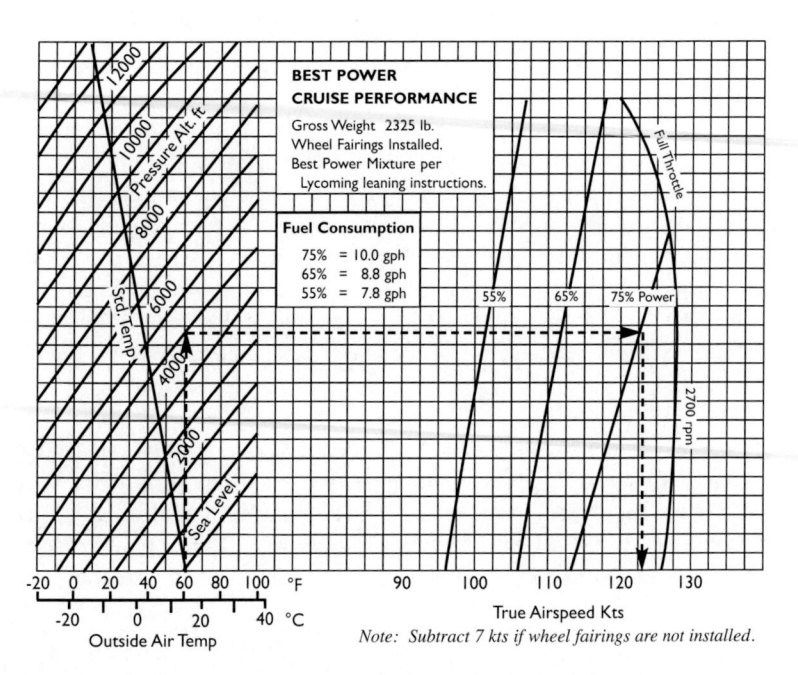

BEST ECONOMY CRUISE PERFORMANCE

Best Economy Mixture per Lycoming Leaning Instructions.
Gross Weight 2325 lb.
Wheel Fairings Installed.

Fuel Consumption
75% = 8.5 gph
65% = 7.5 gph
55% = 6.6 gph

Note: Subtract 7 kts if wheel fairings are not installed

BEST POWER CRUISE PERFORMANCE

Gross Weight 2325 lb.
Wheel Fairings Installed.
Best Power Mixture per Lycoming leaning instructions.

Fuel Consumption
75% = 10.0 gph
65% = 8.8 gph
55% = 7.8 gph

Note: Subtract 7 kts if wheel fairings are not installed.

It should also be remembered that the performance graphs are produced with the aid of a shiny new propeller as well as a newborn engine. A prop that has seen a bit of action will have a detrimental effect on the performance of the aircraft.

The above performance calculations are only personal suggestions using a typical aircraft as an example. For any flight the POH of the aircraft you intend to fly must be used for in service calculations. Furthermore, if you fly at a club or school you should consult their flying order book and/or the CFI recommendations for your aircraft.

Mass and Balance

Preamble and definition of terms:
As mentioned in the performance section, the performance of an aircraft can be seriously affected if it is not loaded in the correct manner. That is, firstly ensure that the aircraft does not exceed the maximum authorised weight. Secondly, ensure that the weight is distributed in such a way that the centre of gravity is retained within the prescribed limits set out in the flight manual. An aircraft operated in excess of its maximum authorised weight would display the following reduction in performance:

> Higher takeoff speed
> Longer takeoff run
> Reduced rate of climb
> Reduced service ceiling
> Reduced cruise performance
> Higher stalling speed
> Increased landing speed
> Increased landing run

To mention only the main items affected. Obviously, the greater the overload the greater the effect will become. Reflecting on AIC 67/2002 we can see a factor that could be applied for increased weight, but this does not mean that you can overload your aircraft so long as you factor in an adjustment for it! Maximum authorised weight is maximum authorised weight. As for balance, or the position of the C of G of an aircraft, this too will affect the aircraft in many ways to the detriment of the handling qualities and performance if not located in the correct position. An aircraft loaded so as to have the C of G outside the forward limit will:

> Require a large elevator down force to balance
> Increase drag as a result
> Increase stalling speed
> Reduce cruise performance
> Reduce nose pitch up available

If outside the rearward limit:

> A spin would be more stable, therefore more difficult to recover
> Reduce longitudinal stability
> Aircraft would tend to pitch up, leading to possible stall on takeoff

These effects, as well as others, would contribute to make life very difficult for the unwary pilot. So it is crucial that as commander and person responsible, the pilot carries out the calculations necessary to ensure the aircraft is not overloaded and that the C of G is in an acceptable position. This is not only for performance reasons but legal as well. The pilot has a legal obligation to operate the aircraft within the manufacturers and regulatory bodies' (e.g. CAA) limitations. If it is not, then the C of A will become invalid. Henceforth, following any incident that may occur the insurance company concerned may fail to pay up, leaving you liable for costs incurred. Following any accident, the weight and balance of the aircraft is likely to be one of the first things an accident investigator will check. Even, if at first, it did not appear to be a contributory factor it would still be a breach of the ANO and cause for the insurance company to discharge any claim or sue you for their losses. You also risk possible prosecution from the CAA. Avoiding all of this nastiness is really quite simple though, just complete a proper weight and balance check on the aircraft you intend to fly. As with the performance calculations, the best way to describe the process is by completing a sample weight and balance schedule.

Mass:
On the surface of the earth, weight is the resultant of the effect of earth's gravity on a particular mass. Therefore, as far as we are concerned they are one and the same thing.

Centre of Gravity (C of G):
Is that point through which the force of gravity can be considered to act on a body.

Moment:
A turning moment, commonly referred to as moment, is the resultant force of a mass multiplied by its distance from its turning point. If two people, of equal weight, sat on a seesaw equidistant from the pivot, they would be in balance. The turning moments would be equal and opposite. We could also say that the centre of gravity of the seesaw was at the pivot point (ignoring the supporting structure). However, if either person moved or their weight changed then the balance would be disturbed and the position of the C of G would move. It is only by analysing the change in the turning moments (Mass x Distance) that we can calculate the new position of the C of G. The new balance point would indeed be our new centre of gravity position. Hence our interest in mass and balance.

The turning moments are equal and opposite, therefore the C of G would be in the centre (i.e. at the balance point). In calculating the C of G of an aircraft, the lever arm distances are measured from a datum specified by the manufacturer together with actual weights of items concerned (e.g. pilot, fuel etc). A weighing report provides the C of G of the basic empty aircraft and it is the responsibility of the pilot to calculate the C of G of the loaded aircraft.

Lever Arm:
   Distance that a mass is removed from its pivot point. Used to calculate a moment.

Station:
   Term sometimes used to describe lever arm.

Datum:
   Vertical plane from which horizontal distances (lever arms) are measured.

Maximum Take-Off Weight:
   Maximum weight approved for the start of the takeoff run.

Basic Empty Weight:
   Weight of empty aircraft, including unusable fuel, full operating fluids, full engine oil. (Does not include disposable load or variable load).

Variable Load:
   Pilot. (Minimum of one!).

Disposable Load:
   Fuel, passengers and baggage.

The first item to work out is the actual weight of the loaded aircraft in the condition you intend to fly it. This requires the simple addition of the weight of the aircraft itself and all you intend putting into it. An example of this is in the Warrior flight manual, set out in tabular form, which is the traditional way. A sample table is illustrated below. Be careful when entering data as the units used vary. Being of American origin generally the flight manuals use imperial units of measure (i.e. pounds and inches). All calculations must be carried out using the same units and not a mix, then, converted if necessary at the end. In the example below we will use lbs and ins, as later we will see that these units are used in our sample flight manual centre of gravity envelope with which we will compare our figures. Some useful conversion figures are included at the end of the book should they be required. The CRP and similar "computers" (circular slide rule would be more correct) and modern electronic navigation calculators will also produce the conversions, provided they are used correctly. However, it is paramount that the pilot have some idea of the results expected when carrying out these calculations and not to believe blindly what the calculator or computer displays as an end result. The awful mish-mash of units that the pilot mathematician has to deal with is the proverbial "accident waiting to happen". To help prevent this develop an ability to estimate closely the result of your diligently worked out calculations that we will go through below.

Mentioning the topic of unit confusion reminds me of an incident involving a large passenger jet aircraft that ran out of fuel in mid journey. (I cannot remember, it is not important, the exact details or those responsible, it is the general lesson that should be learnt.) The aircraft in question obviously required a certain amount of fuel for its journey and this was calculated in kilos. Unfortunately the refuellers equipment was calibrated to show a different unit (pounds maybe, or gallons), the result was that the aircraft only received about half the fuel it required. The ultimate outcome of this was a rather large glider that, at the hands of the very skilled pilots, made a successful forced landing on a disused airbase, much to the relief of the passengers on board. In all calculations take care with the units used.

Sample Mass and Balance Calculation

We begin with the aircraft weighing schedule. This will detail the actual aircraft weight to be used in the loading table, as the basic empty weight. Note, every aircraft weight will be different and the actual weight of your aircraft must be used. Below this, the pilot and passenger weights, fuel weight and any baggage weight are entered into the table. Having done that it should look something like that shown below. So, starting with the weights only, enter these into the table and calculate the total, otherwise known as the maximum all up weight (MAUW) of the aircraft.

Sample Loading Table

Item	Weight (lbs)	Lever Arm (ins)	Moment (lbs x ins)
Basic A/c empty	1501.0	29.9	35940
Pilot		320.0	
Passenger		290.0	
Fuel (80 ltr)		288.0	
Baggage area	10.0		
Total	2409.0		

Maximum Take-off Weight 2325 (normal category)
Maximum Take-off Weight 2020 (utility category)

From the table the total reveals that this would be over weight by 84lbs in the normal category. So, unless pilot or passenger goes on a rather rapid diet and we leave the baggage behind, it demonstrates that we cannot take full fuel. Therefore, we need to reduce the fuel load by 84lbs. This is a case where care needs to be taken to work in the correct units. Fuel weight can be taken as 7.2 lbs per Imp gal, 0.72 Kg per ltr or 6lbs per US gal. As fuel is usually purchased in litres we will need to know how much is required in those units. Avgas fuel density is taken as .72, for weight calculations. Maximum usable fuel is 48 US gals (181.7 ltr), which corresponds to 288 lbs.

Therefore, the maximum fuel weight for this particular trip would be:

$$288 - 84 = 204 \text{ lbs}$$

Converting lbs to US gals:

$$204 \div 6 = 34 \text{ US gals}$$

Which, rather conveniently, is volume in the tanks when filled to the metal tab that protrudes down into the tank from the filler neck for the very purpose! From the quite average adult weights entered in the table it should be apparent that filling the fuel tanks to "tabs" is a normal limitation when four adults are to be carried.

Returning to our example, we can now enter the revised fuel weight that will return the aircraft to within the maximum take-off limit.

Item	Weight (lbs)	Lever Arm (ins)	Moment (lbs x ins)
Basic A/c empty	1501.0	86.49	129 821
Pilot & Front Passenger	320.0	80.5	25 760
Rear Seat Passenger	290.0	118.11	34 249
Fuel (max 48 US gal)	204.0	95.0	19 380
Baggage area	10.0	142.8	1 428
Total	2325.0		210 638

To calculate the centre of gravity (or lever arm) of the loaded aircraft divide the total moment by the total weight:

$$210{,}638 \div 2325 = 90.60 \text{ ins}$$

We now need to check that this is within the permitted range by plotting the information on the centre of gravity limits or moment envelope graphs.

Using the total weight and C of G position we can see that the aircraft has been loaded within the limits of the envelope outlined on the graph and therefore safe to fly.

Sample only - not for operational use.

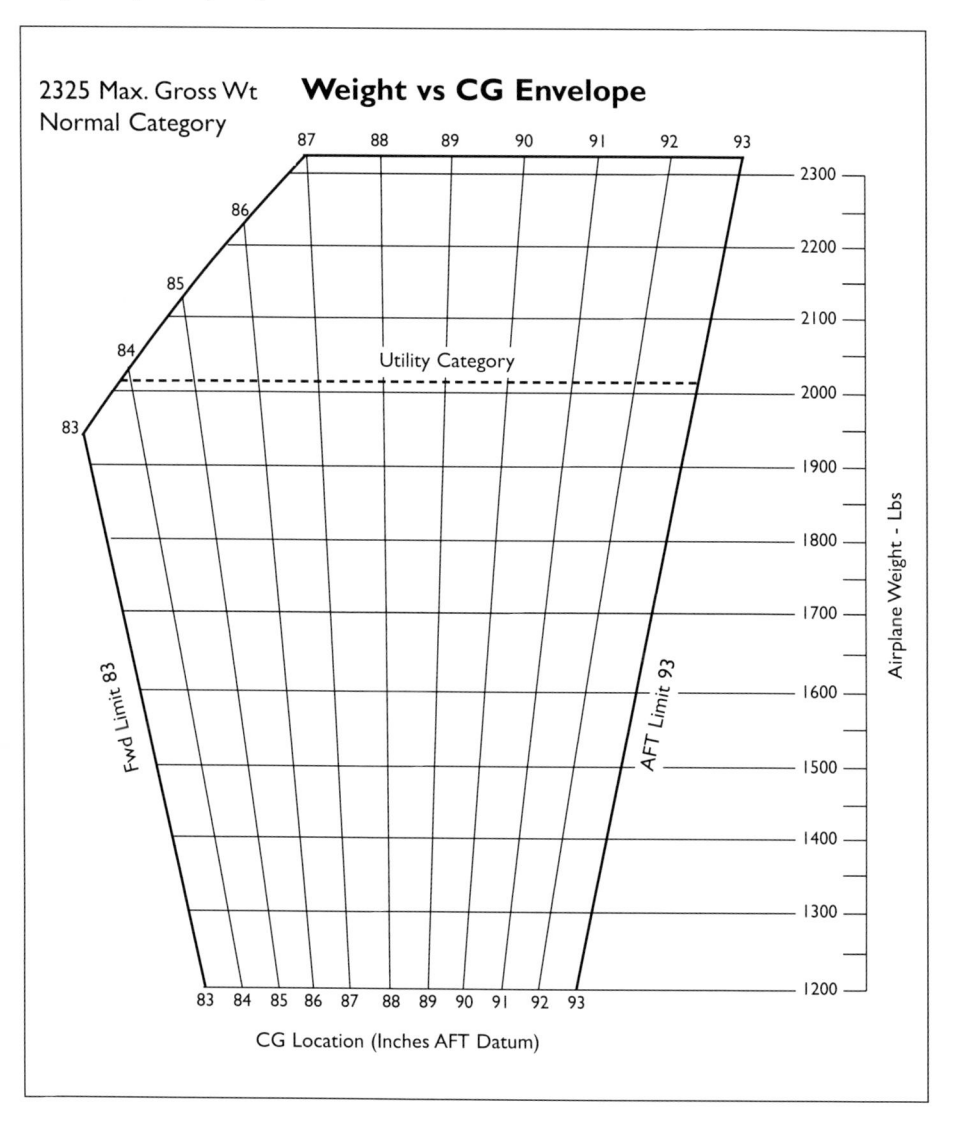

Weight vs CG Envelope

2325 Max. Gross Wt
Normal Category

Utility Category

Fwd Limit 83

AFT Limit 93

Airplane Weight - Lbs

CG Location (Inches AFT Datum)

Note: *No baggage allowed in the baggage compartment if operating in the utility category.*

If the C of G had proved to be outside the limits then we would have to consider ways in which to get it back inside the envelope, which would entail moving the position of, or changing, a particular weight.

With the information available in the Warrior flight manual it is possible to obtain values for the moment of each station directly from the loading graph, shown below, which reduces the work required to fill in a loading table. To use the loading simply enter the weight of a particular station on the vertical axis, plot across to the appropriate reference line (e.g. pilot and front passenger) then vertically down to read off the moment. This effectively carries out the multiplication done in the table.

Sample only - not for operational use.

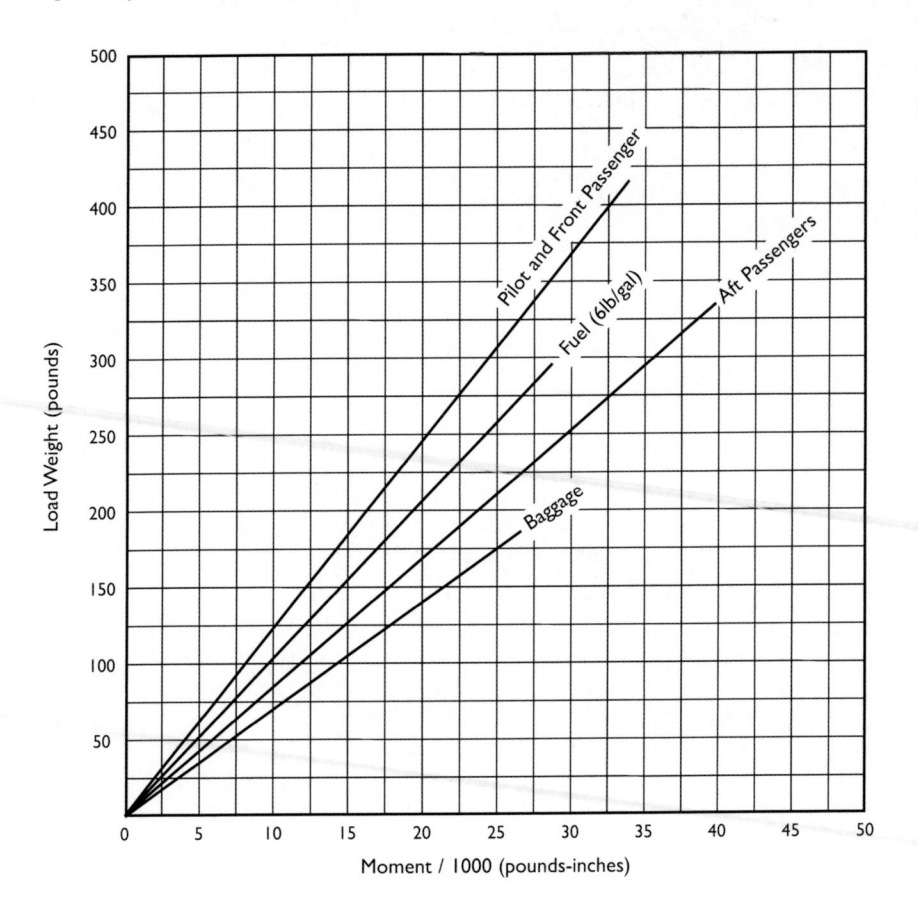

The moments obtained from this graph are entered into the loading table and added together as before to obtain a total moment. The process above is then used to obtain the centre of gravity position, which is then used, together with the total weight, to plot the result on the centre of gravity envelope graph. Note when using this graph the total value for the moments has been divided by 1000 to keep the numbers small.

Using the loading graph is a lot quicker but a little less accurate, so if in doubt, recheck using a table and calculation method to be on the safe side. Any of the foregoing is only an example and not for operational use. Always use the flight manual information that applies to your particular aircraft for calculations, as each one will vary from another similar Warrior and quite different from an Archer or Cadet. The weight and balance schedule will normally be provided by the maintenance organisation responsible for the aircraft and be inserted in the flight manual. Other minor weight variations can occur due to differing levels of radio equipment fitted. For those of you that are a bit wizard on a computer and are familiar with Excel or similar, you can reproduce the weight and balance graphs in these programs and plot directly on to them letting the computer do the work! Nothing like plastic brains eh! But beware, garbage in, garbage out!

Typical Speeds and Limitations

		Warrior and Cadet Kts	Archer Kts
Take-off	(normal, rotate)	50 - 55	57 - 69
	(short field, 25° flap)	48 - 53	55 - 63
Climb	Best rate (Vy)(zero flap)	79	79
	Best angle (Vx)(zero flap)	65	65
	Cruise climb	85	90
Cruise	Normal 2300rpm	105	115
	Safe slow 2000 (25° flap)	80	80
Glide	Best range (0° flap)	73	76
	Best endurance (0° flap)	66-70	66-70
Approach	Normal	70 (Vat 65)	70 (Vat 65)
	Glide	73	76
	Flapless	75	75
	Short Field (Full flap)	63	65

Note: Always check for POH for figures as there are slight variations between specific types.

In strong winds and turbulence it would be advisable to add 5kts to the take-off and landing speeds and consider reducing flap settings.

Maximum demonstrated crosswind   17Kts

To calculate crosswind component either use the table below or the method described earlier, using the imaginary watch face.

Crosswind Angle	10	20	30	40	50	60	70	80	90
Crosswind Factor	0.2	0.3	0.5	0.6	0.7	0.8	0.9	0.9	1.0

Multiply wind speed by crosswind factor to get crosswind component.

Maximum Airspeeds

Maximum Airspeeds (Kts)	Warrior & Cadet	Archer
Maximum Speed Permitted (Vne)	160	154
Maximum Structural Cruising Speed (Vno)	126	125
Maximum Manoeuvring Speed (Va)(@2325lbs) (@1531lbs)	111 86	(@2550)113 (@1634) 89
Maximum Speed Flaps Extended (Vfe)	103	102
Maximum Authorised Take off Weight: (MATW) Normal category Utility category	2325 or 2440lbs 2020lbs	2550lbs 2130lbs

Stall Speeds (Indicated airspeeds given in knots)

Warrior and Cadet

1. At MATW

Flap Deflection	Angle of Bank			
	0°	30°	45°	60°
Up	50	55	60	71
25°	45	48	54	63
40°	44	47	52	61

Archer

2. At MATW

Flap Deflection	Angle of Bank			
	0°	30°	45°	60°
Up	54	59	64	76
25°	49	53	59	69
40°	48	50	56	66

Airspeed Indicator Colour Coding (speeds in Kts)

	Warrior & Cadet	Archer
Red line Vne	160	154
Yellow arc (caution range)	126 - 160	125 - 154
Green arc (normal ops range)	50 - 126	55 - 125
White arc (flap operating range)	44 - 103	49 - 102

Structural Load Limitations

Cadet, Warrior & Archer

Maximum Positive Load Factor:	Normal	3.8G
	Utility	4.4G

Maximum Negative Load Factor: No inverted manoeuvres approved.

Flight by Night: The aircraft is approved for flight by night. Providing the minimum equipment for flight at night (see ANO, schedule 5) is serviceable.

Flight in Icing Conditions: Flight in icing conditions is strictly prohibited.

Other Useful Figures

Typical Engine

Warrior	Lycoming 0-320-D2A/D3G	160hp @ 2700rpm
Archer	Lycoming 0-320-A4M	180hp @ 2700rpm
Engine RPM:	Max RPM	2700 (Red line)
Normal Operating Range:		500-2700rpm (Green arc)
	(Archer)	500-2650rpm (Green arc)
Oil Capacity:		8 US quarts (7.6ltr)
	Min safe	2 US quarts (1.9ltr)
Oil Temperature:	Max	118°C/245F (Red line)
	Normal range	75F -245F (Green arc)
Oil Pressure:	Warrior Max	100psi (Red line)
	(Archer Max)	90psi (Red line)
	Normal range	60-90psi (Green arc)
	Minimum idling	25psi (Red line)
	Caution range (idle)	25-60psi (Yellow arc)
	Caution range	90-100psi (Yellow arc)
	(Ground warm up - Warrior II only)	

Fuel System

Fuel Grade:	100LL Aviation grade (Blue)
	100 Aviation grade (Green)

Capacities
Total fuel:	50US gals (189.3ltr)
Usable fuel:	48US gals (181.7ltr)
Unusable fuel:	2US gals (7.6ltr)
When filled to tabs:	34US gals (128.7ltr)

Fuel Pressure
Minimum	0.5psi (Red line)
Maximum	8.0psi (Red line)
Normal operating range	0.5 - 8.0 (Green arc)

Tyres

Warrior II and Cadet
Nose Wheel (6.00 × 6)	pressure 30psi
Main Wheels (6.00 × 6)	pressure 24psi

Archer II
Nose Wheel (6.00 × 6)	pressure 18psi
Main Wheels (6.00 × 6)	pressure 24psi

Piper Warrior Pre-Flight Check List

Check lists are an essential part of a pilot's equipment, and their importance cannot be over emphasised. Whilst in flight checks should be committed to memory, as these are relatively few, the checks required before getting airborne should rigorously follow the approved checklist. Never rush the checks, work at your own pace steadily through each line in the checklist. Also, beware of any line in a check list that has more than one item, as the second item can easily be missed and subsequently not checked; especially if you feel under pressure to get the job done. The checks actually begin before you get to the aircraft. First of all check that all the paperwork is in order and that the aircraft has enough hours left for your flight before the next service check. With that done and the correct flight authorisation complete, on approaching the aircraft take a distant view of the way it is parked and how it appears to stand on the ground. Does it stand level? Does it list to one side or perhaps looks rather nose low. Either may be due to the terrain it is parked on or indicate some other problem. If parked on soft ground (e.g. grass in winter time) it may have sunk in a bit and it would be prudent to push the aircraft forward out of the depressions before attempting to taxi. Also make a note of the condition of the area in which you intend to taxi if it is a grass surface, which can obscure all manner of nasty surprises for the unwary! Rabbit holes, old tie downs left behind, even ill placed taxiway lights seem to have an amazingly magnetic attraction to an aircraft when you get distracted by your passenger or someone else wittering at you through the headset. With this in mind we can begin with our more detailed checks.

Ensure that any tie downs, external control locks, wheel chocks and pitot cover are removed and stored securely. It may appear highly amusing to bystanders to watch you try and taxi off whilst still firmly attached to the ground and with a low wing type the tie downs could be missed if you carry out an abridged form of walk round.

Aircraft Tie-down Point

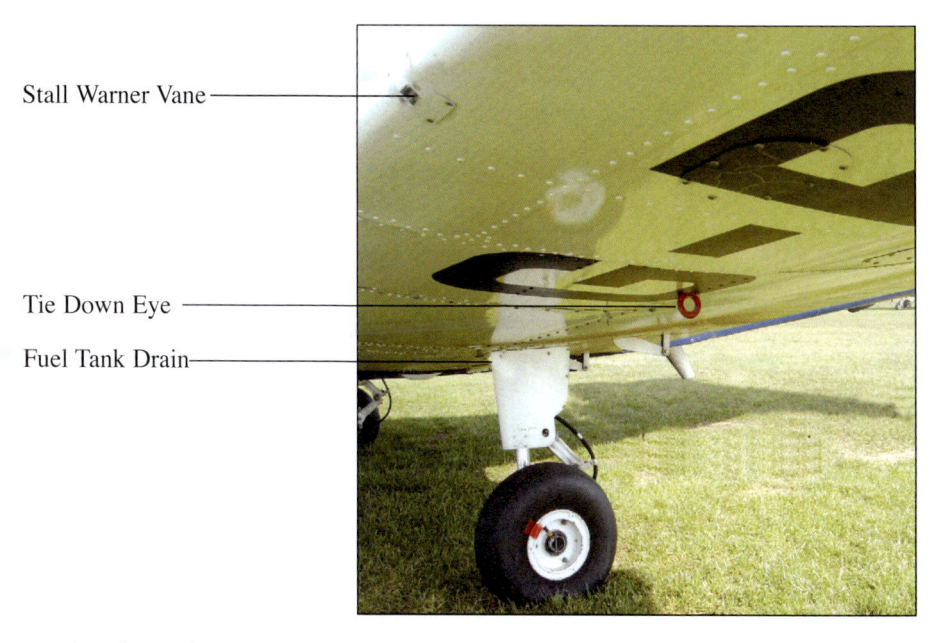

Stall Warner Vane

Tie Down Eye

Fuel Tank Drain

Any ice or frost must be removed from all surfaces. Special care should be taken with the Perspex windows as these can be damaged very easily. Do not use a credit card scraper!

Remove aircraft cover, if fitted, folding from the back to the front leaving the part behind the spinner until last; then it will be the first part to secure when refitting. This makes it easier if you are refitting the cover on your own when the wind is blowing. Provided, of course, that you have parked into wind! With that done proceed into the cabin to start the checks.

In Cabin:

Remove any control locks and stow securely.
Park brake on.
Check First Aid kit sealed and secure. (If not sealed a vital part might be missing)
Check fire extinguisher secure and pressure reading in green arc.
Magnetos OFF and key out.
Avionics master switch (if fitted) OFF.
Check all radios and all other electrical equipment are switched off.
Master switch on: Check fuel gauges rising (note contents indicated)
    Turn on: Anti-collision beacon and strobes (if fitted)
                       Pitot heater
                       Navigation lights
                       Landing lights
Exit cabin and check all items switched on for serviceability in turn (pitot will take a short while to warm up so check this last).
Stall warner vane can be gently lifted to check operation.
Return to cockpit. Turn off electrical equipment listed above
Master switch OFF.
Fuel selector; turn on (select tank with least contents).
Trimmer; select neutral position.
Pitot/Static drains; operate.
Lower Flaps (Fully down, check all stages).
Exit cabin and beware not to tread on the flap surface.

Cabin Upper Fuselage

Close cabin door and check door security.
Starboard windows, clean and undamaged.
Upper fuselage; skin undamaged, any aerials undamaged and secure
Tow bar (if used) stowed securely.
Baggage door, secure.
Proceed around aircraft in an anticlockwise direction.

Starboard Wing

Flap: Check upper and lower surface condition linkages and hinges secure and greased. If operating from grass airfields, check for mud stuck to the lower and forward surfaces.

Aileron: Check upper and lower surface condition linkages and hinges secure and greased. Mass balance. Drain holes clear. Aileron should be smooth in movement requiring little force. Take care with fingers inside the hinge line when checking operation. (Prevent movement with other hand).

Wing Tip: Undamaged and secure, nav light (green) and strobe unbroken.

Wing Surface: Upper, lower surface and leading edge undamaged and generally clean.

Fuel Tank: Check contents and correctly secure cap. Operate fuel drain valve into appropriate container; check for dirt, water and correct colour, repeat if necessary. (First flight of day and after refuelling). After use ensure that fuel drain is closed and not dripping. Check fuel tank vent is clear.

Fresh Air Vent: Clear.

Starboard Undercarriage

Security and Condition of Brake Caliper and Pads: Caliper is semi-floating type so will have a certain amount of play when checked. Pads should not be worn down to metal backing plate.

Security and Condition of Brake Disc: Should not be loose, rusty or pitted.

Hydraulic Lines: Check for damage and leaks, particularly adjacent to the calliper.

Wheel & Tyre: Check for general wear, damage, alignment of creep marks and correct inflation.

Leg and Fairing (if fitted): Check general condition, particularly security of wheel fairing and if conditions are conducive, check for mud filling the fairing.

Oleo: Check extension (4.5").

Front Fuselage, Engine and Nose Leg

Windscreen: Check clean and undamaged. OAT probe secure.

Starboard Cowling: Open to check oil contents (recommend min 5qts), do not overtighten dipstick on refitting. Visually inspect general condition of components in the engine bay. Re-secure cowling ensuring catches have fastened correctly. (Note, the Archer only provides access to the oil dipstick through a small hatch in the cowling).

Nose Leg: Oleo extension (3.25"), linkages, nuts and split pins secure and no signs of oil leakage.

Nose Wheel: Check for correct tyre inflation, no damage and creep marks aligned.

Propeller and Spinner: Treat live at all times. Check for cracks or nicks especially along the leading edge and spinner for condition and security.
DO NOT TURN THE PROPELLER.

Front Cowling: Check condition and security. Air intakes clear, alternator belt tension correct and landing light undamaged.

Port Cowling: Open and check brake fluid reservoir for correct fluid level. Further general check of engine components for obvious defects. Re-secure cowling and take fuel sample from strainer drain if appropriate, ensure drain is closed and not leaking after use.

Port Undercarriage: Security and condition of brake calliper and pads. Caliper is semi-floating type so will have a certain amount of play when checked. Pads should not be worn down to metal backing plate.

Security and Condition of Brake Disc: Should not be loose, rusty or pitted.

Hydraulic Lines: Check for damage and leaks, particularly adjacent to the caliper.

Wheel and Tyre:	Check for general wear, damage, alignment of creep marks and correct inflation.
Leg and Fairing (if fitted):	Check general condition, particularly security of wheel fairing and if conditions are conducive, check for mud filling the fairing.
Oleo:	Check extension (4.5").

Port Wing

Fresh Air Vent:	Clear.
Fuel Tank:	Check contents and correctly secure cap. Operate fuel drain valve into appropriate container; check for dirt, water and correct colour, repeat if necessary. (First flight of day and after refuelling). After use ensure that fuel drain is closed and not dripping. Check fuel tank vent is clear.
Wing Surface:	Upper, lower surface and leading edge undamaged and generally clean.
Pressure Head:	Check pitot and static vent are unobstructed. (Do not blow into vents).
Stall Warning Vane:	Free and undamaged.
Wing Tip:	Undamaged and secure, nav light (red) and strobe unbroken.
Aileron:	Check upper and lower surface condition; linkages and hinges secure and greased. Mass balance. Drain holes clear. Aileron should be smooth in movement requiring little force. Take care with fingers inside the hinge line when checking operation. (Prevent movement with other hand).
Flap:	Check upper and lower surface condition; linkages and hinges secure and greased. If operating from grass airfields, check for mud stuck to the lower and forward surfaces.

Port Fuselage, Fin and Rudder

Fuselage Skin and Windows: Clean and undamaged.

Fin Surface: Secure and undamaged (including fairings). Condition and security of rotating beacon and any fin mounted aerials (e.g. VOR).

Rudder: Surface undamaged. Hinge bolts and operating linkage secure and greased. Check navigation light (white) unbroken. Do not try and force rudder movement and do not touch rudder trim tab.

Stabilator: Check upper and lower surface condition; linkages and hinges secure and greased. Carefully check full and free movement without using too much force. Check movement and linkage of anti-balance tab.

Check Starboard Side of Rear Fuselage: Clean and undamaged.

Internal and Pre Start Checks

1. **Flap:** Up
2. **Seat:** Adjusted and secure.
3. **Harness:** Lap and shoulder strap adjusted and secure.
3. **Cabin Door:** Closed and latched
4. **Parking Brake:** On.
5. **Alternate Static Source:** Check normal
6. **Instruments:** Undamaged, legible and secure. Compass and deviation card
7. **Cabin Air/Heat:** Free movement of controls and set closed.
8. **Fuel:** Check on least full tank.
9. **Circuit Breakers:** Check all in
10. **Trim:** Check full and free movement, in correct sense and set for take off.
11. **Controls:** Full and free movement in correct sense.
12. **Master Switch:** On. (If night nav lights on)
    Annunciator/low voltage light: Check/on
    VAC off caption: On
13. **Radios:** Off. (Unless start up clearance or airfield data required. Ensure off for start up)

14. Altimeter: Set as required. (Aerodrome QNH if departing, QFE for circuit, if setting not obtained set to zero should show anticipated QFE, set to airfield elevation the QNH, both +50, -75ft)
15. Beacon: On.

Starting

1. Mixture: Full and free movement. Set to fully rich.
2. Throttle: Full and free movement. Set to ¼ " open.
3. Carb Heat Control: Full and free movement. Set to cold
4. Fuel Pump: Check operation then off.
5. Primer: Prime as required and lock

6. LOOKOUT: Check all round aircraft, open DV window, **shout** clear prop. Cover brakes.
7. Magnetos: Key in, (hand on throttle) turn to start position.

After Start

1. Starter Warner Light: Out, if not, immediately turn the magneto switch to stop the engine.
2. Oil Pressure: Rising to green arc within 30 secs (If not, mag switch off).
3. RPM: Set 1200 rpm as normal idle engine speed.
4. Alternator: On (check load on ammeter).
5. Low voltage light: Out
6. Suction: Check 3" to 5" (green arc). VAC off caption light out.
7. Radios: On and tuned to correct frequencies. (Obtain ATIS or airfield data). Check intercom function adjust if necessary.
8. Instruments: Set D.I. and Alt. Check A.I. erected. Turn Co-ord. flag away.
9. Magnetos: Dead cut check at 1200rpm. (Looking for a drop no stop, if engine is still cold it may not run particularly smoothly on one mag at this stage).
10. Annunciator Panel: Lights all out/test.
11. Electric Trim: Check operation and then off.

12. **Avionics:** Set as required.
13. **Radio:** Turn up volume and listen out Request radio check and (if required) taxi clearance.

Taxying

1. **Brakes:** Close throttle, release brakes. Increase power sufficiently to move forward then close throttle and gently test brakes.
2. **Rudder:** Check directional control.
3. **Instruments:** During turns check compass and D.I. turning correctly and in same direction. Turn co-ordinator showing a turn in the correct direction and the ball a skid. Attitude indicator level.
4. **Wind Direction:** Note the wind direction relative to taxi direction and hold the control column in the appropriate position. Be aware of weathercock action in strong crosswind.

Power Checks

1. **Position:** Into wind, clear of rough ground, loose stones, personnel and other aircraft. Also that subsequent propwash will not adversely affect other a/c especially tail wheel types.
2. **Brakes:** On, but covered as well.
3. **Fuel:** Change to fuller tank.
4. **Oil:** Temperature and pressure steady and within limits.
5. **Rpm:** Check clear all round. Set to 2000 rpm.
6. **Carb Heat:** Operate to hot position, should show approx 50-75 rpm drop, return to cold position.
7. **Magnetos:** Check each magneto in turn. Max permissible drop 175rpm, max differential is 50rpm. Ensure after check mags on both.
8. **Suction:** Between 4.9 and 5.1"Hg or in the green arc.
9. **Alternator:** Check output.
10. **Oil:** Temperature and pressure steady and within limits.
11. **Throttle** Smoothly close the throttle and check rpm 500-700. Recheck oil temp. and pressure as above. Reset to 1200.

Pre Take Off Checks

1. **T**   Trim control set for take off
2. **T**   Throttle friction nut finger tight
3. **M**   Mixture rich
4. **C**   Carb Heat cold. (Recheck if take off delayed)
5. **M**   Master switch on
6. **M**   Magnetos on both
7. **F**   Fuel on fuller tank and sufficient
8. **F**   Fuel pump on
9. **P**   Primer in and locked
10. **F**   Flaps as required
11. **G**   Gauges, oil temp and pressure in limits
12. **I**   Instruments, D.I. set. Alt. set
13. **R**   Radios, set as required
14. **H**   Harnesses secure
15. **H**   Hatches, doors and windows secure
16. **P**   Pitot heat, as required
17. **C**   Controls, all full and free movement
18. **T**   Take off brief. Review speeds, assess crosswind effect and control. Establish emergency procedures.

Take Off

Normal Take off:

1. Lookout: Obtain clearance, check approach path clear visually.
2. Line up: On runway centre line, ensure nosewheel straight.
                  Check D.I. indicating runway heading
3. Brakes: Off, heels on the floor.
4. Throttle: Smoothly open to full power.
5. Oil: Temperature and pressure steady in green arc.
6. Airspeed: Increasing at 50kts use elevator, raise nose. Lift off at 55kts
                  Climb at 79kts (clean).

After Take Off:

1. Lookout: Point selected left of nose. Check drift!
                  (Maintain any noise abatement procedure.)
2. Flaps: Retract above 200ft, not below 60kts.
3. Oil: Temperature and pressure steady and within limits.
4. Departure: As per ATC instructions or brief.

Climb

Normal Climb:

1. Airspeed: Clean 79kts for best rate of climb (Best angle 65kts).
2. Throttle: Full open
3. Mixture: Full rich below 3000ft

En-route Climb:

1. Airspeed: 85Kts
2. Throttle: Full open
3. Mixture: Full rich below 3000ft

Cruise:

1. Airspeed: 100 -115kts (dependent on model and power set, alt etc)
2. Power: 2200 - 2600rpm (dependent on temp and alt check cruise/eng perf graph).
3. Elevator Trim: Adjust as required.
4. Mixture: Lean as per recommendations.

En-route Checks: FREDA

F Fuel   - Check contents/tank selection.
R Radios   - Com. Check volume. Change frequency if reqd.
                  Nav. Check freq and ident as reqd
E Engine   - Check for carb icing. Check oil temperature and pressure.
                  Ammeter charging. Suction within limits. Mixture as reqd.
D D.I.   - Synchronised with compass.
A Altimeter - Set as required.

Pre Stall Checks: HASELL

H Height   - Sufficient to recover by 2500ft a.g.l.
A Airframe - Flaps as required for stalling. Brakes off.
S Security - Doors, and harness secure. No loose articles.
                  Check fire extinguisher fastened in place.
E Engine   - Check oil temperature and pressure. Mixture as required.
                  Clear any carb ice. Check fuel contents.
L Location - Check clear of:
                  A - Active airfields
                  B - Built up areas
                  C - Cloud or controlled airspace
                  D - Danger areas
L LOOKOUT - Carry out a 180° or two 90° turns to check no other aircraft around or below.

Between successive manoeuvres (e.g. stalls) the HELL elements of the check are normally sufficient. Note: reset DI following the completion of the exercise.

On approach to an airfield carry out a FREDA check, setting mixture to rich and Altimeter to QFE when field is in sight.

Pre Landing: BUMPFFICHH

B	Brakes	-	Off, pressure check
U	Undercarriage	-	Fixed
M	Mixture	-	Rich
P	Propeller Pitch	-	Fixed
F	Fuel	-	On fullest tank sufficient for "Go Around".
F	Fuel pump	-	On.
I	Instruments	-	Engine gauges normal. Altimeter set (QFE). DI set
C	Carb Heat	-	Check for icing then return to cold.
H	Harnesses	-	Check pilot and passengers.
H	Hatches	-	Check doors and DV window.

Landing

Normal Landing:

1. Carb heat: Apply full heat before reducing power.
2. Flaps: Select 25° when speed is below 102kts
   (Full flap on final approach).
3. Airspeed: Adjust attitude for 70kts and trim.
   Reduce to 65kts at the threshold.
4. Touchdown: Hold off to touchdown on main wheels first, then lower nose wheel gently.
5. Braking: Minimum required for runway length.

Flapless Landing:

1. Airspeed: 70-75kts
2. Braking: More braking may be required due to higher landing speed.

Shortfield Landing:

1. Flaps   Full flap on final approach.
2. Airspeed   65kts (63kts at threshold)
3. Touchdown   Main wheels first, lower nose wheel promptly.
4. Braking   Apply positively (beware of wheel lock).

Glide Approach:

1. Airspeed   Flaps up   75kts
                Flaps 25°   70kts
                Flaps 40°   70kts

Notes: During prolonged glides the engine should be warmed every 500ft. The approach speeds are for calm conditions, in gusty or turbulent conditions the speeds should be increased accordingly

Go- Around (Overshoot)

1. Throttle   Full power (control pitch and yaw)
2. Carb Heat   Select cold position.
3. Airspeed   Adjust attitude for 65kts
4. Flaps   If 40°, retract to 25° as soon as possible. Retract remaining 25° when above 200ft and positive rate of climb. Continue clean climb at 79kts.
5. Radio   Inform ATC.

After Landing

Taxi clear of runway and stop the aircraft:

1. Carb heat   Cold.
2. Flaps   Up.
3. Pitot heat   Off.
4. Throttle   Throttle friction nut loose.
5. Lights   Strobe and landing lights off.
6. Transponder   Standby.
7. Trim   Neutral
8. Other electrics   Non-essentials off

Shut Down

1. Park   Into wind, nosewheel straight.
2. Parking brake   On.
3. Engine   Idle for at least 30secs at 1200, check oil temperature and pressure.
4. Magnetos   Dead cut check.
5. Radios   Com and nav off.
6. Mixture   Lean to I.C.O.
7. Throttle   Closed.

After Engine Stops:

1. Magnetos   Off, key out.
2. Beacon   Off
3. Nav lights   Off
4. Master switch   Off
5. Fuel   Off
6. Harnesses   Left tidy
7. External   Secure door. Pitot cover on (if available). Tie down and/or fit chocks if necessary.

EMERGENCIES

FIRE ON THE GROUND: During Engine Start

1. Continue cranking for the time required for the rest of procedure.
2. Mixture   -   I.C.O.
3. Fuel   -   OFF.
4. Master switch   -   OFF.
5. Magnetos   -   OFF.
6. Exit aircraft with fire extinguisher and direct contents onto base of fire.

If fire continues abandon and keep well clear.

FIRE IN THE AIR: Engine Fire:

1. Fuel   -   OFF.
2. Throttle   -   Closed.
3. Mixture   -   I.C.O.
4. Electric fuel pump -   OFF.
5. Cabin heat and air -   OFF (except ankle air vents).
6. Mayday Call
7. Master switch   -   OFF.
8. Magnetos   -   OFF.
9. Speed   -   Set up max rate of descent. Full flap at 102Kts.
10. Side slip if necessary to keep flame and smoke away from cabin.
11. Carry out forced landing procedure.

Cabin Fire:

1. Master switch   -   OFF
2. Air vents   -   Open
3. Fire Extinguisher   -   Use if necessary, but then ventilate cabin well.
4. Land as soon as possible.

Electrical Fire:

1. Master switch   -   OFF
2. All other switches (except ignition)   Off.
3. Air vents   -   Open.
4. Fire Extinguisher   -   Use if necessary, but then ventilate cabin well.

If fire appears to be out and electrical power is required.

5. Master switch   -   ON.
6. Circuit breakers   -   Check, do not reset any that have tripped.
7. Electrics Switch on one circuit at a time carefully, try to identify each one as safe before proceeding to the next.

Engine Failure After Take Off:

1. Lower nose to maintain best gliding speed
2. Close throttle
3. Select the most suitable landing area ahead (the runway if sufficient remains) or around the aircraft bearing in mind the wind direction and any obstacles.
4. Use flap as necessary
5. Mixture   -   I.C.O.
6. Fuel   -   OFF.
7. Magnetos   -   OFF.
8. Mayday call if time permits
9. Master   -   OFF.
10. Harness   -   Tight, unlatch door.

Forced Landing without Power:

1. Adopt glide attitude and trim for correct glide speed.
2. Assess wind velocity.
3. Select a landing area.
4. Plan descent.
5. Carry out engine failure checks:

Fuel	-	Select tank containing fuel.
Fuel pump	-	Switch on.
Mixture	-	Ensure rich.
Throttle	-	Check position.
Carb heat	-	Check and change position.
Magnetos	-	On both.
Primer	-	Locked.
Engine gauges	-	Check for indication of fault.

If no obvious fault found that will rectify situation.

6. Mayday call (A/c call sign, position and route most important)
7. Complete committal drill:

Mixture	-	I.C.O.
Fuel	-	Off.
Throttle	-	Closed.
Magnetos	-	Off.
Brakes	-	Off.
Harness	-	Tight.
Master switch	-	Off.

8. Recheck approach to landing area and adjust as necessary.
9. Use full flap for touchdown if not already fully down.
10. After touchdown stop as soon as possible with heavy braking. Evacuate and move away from the aircraft.

Forced Landing with Power:

1. Assess the time available and check: Fuel state
   Hours of daylight remaining
   Rate of weather deterioration

2. Assess wind velocity.
3. Select suitable landing area
4. Carry out an inspection run at slow safe cruising speed (80kts, flap 25°) initially at around 500ft a.g.l. to for check obstructions.
5. Carry out further inspection run at around 100ft for closer check of approach path and surface condition (if time and conditions permit).
6. Approach using short field technique.
7. After touchdown stop as soon as possible with heavy braking.

Ditching Procedure:

1. Set up minimum rate of descent (65kts).
2. Mayday call.
3. Head towards any shipping.
4. Harness tight.
5. Secure or jettison heavy objects.
6. Unlatch door.
7. Activate E.L.B.
8. If large swell and light wind, land along swell in tail down near stalling attitude. If strong wind and light or heavy swell, land into wind in tail down near stalling attitude.
9. Evacuate aircraft and DO NOT inflate life jackets until outside cabin.

Action in Event of Radio Failure:

1. Check frequency is correct.
2. Check volume setting.
3. Check microphone and headset plugs are in and secure.
4. Adjust squelch setting (if applicable)
5. Check circuit breaker (reset only once).
6. Transmit blind or use PTT switch to try to communicate.

Use appropriate non-radio procedures and obey visual signals. If unaware of exact procedure in circuit, keep clear of other traffic and on final approach flash landing light on and off. Land unless given signal not to.

Electrical Failures:

1. Check circuit breaker not tripped (reset only once).
2. Check master switch on
3. Assess nature of failure (i.e. one circuit of little significance or major that may lead to total electrical failure).
4. If second scenario then reduce electrical load.
5. Notify ATC.
6. Land as soon as practicable.

If all electrics are lost then see above for radio failure.

ALT Annunciator Light Illuminated:

Check ammeter to verify alternator failure.

If ammeter shows zero:

Alternator Switch	-	OFF.
Reduce electrical load to a minimum.		
Alternator circuit breaker	-	Check and reset if necessary.
Alternator switch	-	ON.

If power is not restored:

Alternator switch - OFF.

If alternator output cannot be restored, then maintain minimum electrical load and land as soon as practicable:

Electrical Overload (Ammeter displaying 20 amps in excess of known load)

A/c equipped with interlocked BAT. and ALT. switch:
Reduce electrical load.
If ammeter reading reduces - ALT switch OFF.
Land as soon as practicable.

A/c equipped with separate BAT. and ALT. switches:
Alternator Switch - ON.
Battery Switch - OFF.

> Note: Due to increased system voltage and radio frequency noise, operation with the alternator switch ON and the battery switch OFF should only be carried out when required by an electrical system failure.

If ammeter reading reduces:
Reduce electrical load to min.
Land as soon as practicable.

If ammeter reading does not reduce:
Alternator Switch - OFF.
Battery Switch - As required.

Appendix 1

Glossary of Terms

Some Common V Codes:

Va – Manoeuvring Speed
This is the maximum speed at which you should make any abrupt or full control movements.

Vno – Maximum Structural Cruising Speed
This is the maximum speed at which you can fly in turbulent conditions.

Vne – Never Exceed Speed
This is the maximum speed that you may fly in any circumstances and must not be exceeded.

Vfe – Maximum Speed with Flaps Extended
This is the highest speed allowed to extend the flaps or fly with them extended.

Vs1 – Stalling Speed in clean configuration (ie flaps up) and idle power

Vs0 – Stalling Speed with full flap and idle power.

Vx – Best Angle of Climb
This is the speed at which there will be the greatest gain in altitude in a given horizontal distance.

Vy – Best Rate of Climb.
This is the speed at which there will be the greatest gain in altitude in a given time.

Airspeeds

IAS – Indicated Airspeed This is the speed displayed on the airspeed indicator and normally expressed in knots.

RAS – Rectified Airspeed This is the IAS corrected for instrument and the position of the static vent.

TAS – True Airspeed This is RAS corrected for density.

Appendix 2

Common Abbreviations

AAIB	Air accident investigation branch
A. G. L.	Above ground level
AIC	Aeronautical information circular
ADF	Automatic direction finding.
ANO	Air navigation order
ATC	Air traffic control
BHP	Brake horsepower
CAA	Civil aviation authority
CofG	Centre of Gravity.
CofR	Certificate of Registration
CofA	Certificate of Airworthiness
CofMR	Certificate of Maintenance Review
CofRS	Certificate of Release to Service
DME	Distance measuring equipment.
E. L. B.	Emergency locator beacon.
ICO	Idle cut off.
IFR	Instrument flight rules
MSL	Mean sea level.
POH	Pilots operating handbook.
QFE	Barometric pressure set on altimeter to read height above a datum.
QNH	Barometric pressure set on altimeter to read altitude above MSL
SAE	Society of automobile engineers.
VHF	Very high frequency.
VFR	Visual flight rules

Appendix 3

Glossary of Terms

Anti-balance Tab	Trim tab fitted to rear of stabilator design to work in opposition of movement to induce "feel", or pressure opposing movement of control column.
Cantilever	Unbraced, supported at one end only.
Dihedral	Term used to describe wings that incline upwards from mounting point to wing tip.
Detonation	A too-rapid burning or explosion of the mixture in the cylinders. It becomes audible through a vibration of the combustion chamber walls and is sometimes confused with "pinking" or spark "knock".
Frame	Annular structure, ring of metal extrusion forming the shape of the fuselage. Joined together by the longerons and stringers.
Flutter	Destructive vibration of an aerofoil surface.
Longeron	Metal extrusion of more strength than a stringer joining frames.
Pre-ignition	Ignition occurring earlier than intended. For example, the mixture being fired in the cylinder by a flake of incandescent carbon before the electric spark.
Stabilator	Single all moving horizontal tail surface.
Stringer	Lightweight metal extrusion joining frames.
Torque Tube	A tube with fittings mounted in bearings so that a rotational force can be used to transmit a control input to a flying control surface. (e.g. the flaps)
Wash Out	Slight twist in a wing that reduces angle of incidence towards the tip.

International Standard Atmosphere (ISA)

Conditions at Sea Level:

Temperature	+15°C
Density	1225 gm/ccm
Pressure	1013 Hpa (or mb)
Lapse Rate	1.98°C/1000 ft

Dihedral	Wings that incline upwards from mounting point to wing tip.
Wash out	Slight twist in a wing that reduces angle of incidence towards the tip.
Creep	Movement of tyre around the rim of the wheel, can cause the valve to tear off the inner tube.

Useful Conversion Factors:

Distances
Centimetres to inches	× 0.3937
Inches to centimetres	× 2.54
Metres to feet	× 3.2808
Feet to metres	× 0.3048
Kilometres to nautical miles	× 0.5399
Nautical miles to kilometres	× 1.852

Weights
Kilograms to pounds	× 2.2046
Pounds to kilograms	× 0.4536

Volumes
Litres to imperial gallons	× 0.22
Litres to US gallons	× 0.264
Imperial gallons to litres	× 4.546
Imperial gallons to US gallons	× 1.201
US gallons to litres	× 3.785
US gallons to imperial gallons	× 0.833

Notes

Notes